Scattered Memories

Nicholas Cobbold
with
Clive Hodges

The Cobbold Family History Trust

First published 2015 by The Cobbold Family History Trust

© Nicholas Cobbold, Clive Hodges
and The Cobbold Family History Trust

All rights reserved. Except as permitted under current legislation, no part of this work may be photocopied, stored in a retrieval system, published, performed in public, adapted, broadcast, transmitted, recorded or reproduced in any form or by any means, without the prior permission of the copyright owner.

The right of Nicholas Cobbold and Clive Hodges to be identified as the authors of this work has been asserted in accordance with sections 77 and 78 of the Copyright, Designs and Patents Act 1988.

ISBN 978 0 9932117 9 9

Typeset and project managed by Clive Hodges
Cover design by Alex Williams
Printed by Short Run Press Ltd.

For my family

Contents

Forward by Peter Wilmot-Sitwell   vii

Introduction   ix

1. A Free Range Childhood   1

2. Into the Army   49

3. In the City and in the Country   85

4. To the Skies   117

5. The Middle Years   154

6. Headhunting and Slowing Down   191

Index   211

Foreword *by Peter Wilmot-Sitwell*

Nicholas Cobbold was born in 1934 and spent his childhood at his grandmother's country estate in Wiltshire.

He was educated at Eton and then joined the Coldstream Guards for National Service.

His working life was spent in the City of London and he is renowned for his sense of humour, and has a reputation for being possibly one of the best shots in the country. In 2009, *The Field* compiled a list of the hundred best shots over the previous century. Nicholas' name appears on the list and the citation accompanying the entry reads, 'From the Sixties to 1990 indisputably one of the best on high pheasants.'

Introduction

Arriving at a decision to write one's autobiography is not always easy. This is particularly so if, like me, one is not a public figure or someone who enjoys that rather cheap commodity nowadays, celebrity status. In considering the question 'to write or not to write?' I was mindful of a number of things. Foremost amongst these was the concern that the life I have led has not been sufficiently interesting to bother writing about; that my life story would make dull reading and that such a book might be considered by those who know me as something of an ill-advised vanity project. I confess that, even as the book is now published, I have not completely allayed these concerns.

Weighing against this inhibition was the desire to write a memoir for those closest to me and their expressed desire to have one. Ever since I started to take things a little easier, my children have made occasional calls for me to write a record of my varied life as a keepsake and as something that they can then pass on to their own children and that can then be handed down through future generations. I suppose that most of us, if we were ever to consider the question, would dearly love to have such a memoir of our parents. I think that it is often the case that being so busy in our own lives we do not know as much about our parents as we think we do, particularly when it comes to the early parts of their lives. I hope my children and grandchildren will find one or two surprises here and that some of the stories I tell will cause them to smile from time to time. This book has been written for my family, though I hope that many of the great friends I have made throughout my life may also find parts of it interesting and amusing. Should it appeal to an audience beyond those close to me, I will, indeed, be flattered.

The opportunity to write *Scattered Memories* presented itself in June 2013 when I was introduced to Clive Hodges, an historian with a special interest in the Cobbold family which was sparked when he encountered records at the National Archives of India relating to my grandfather's career as a Great Game spy in central Asia in the late nineteenth century. Clive writes for The Cobbold Family History Trust, which seeks to preserve all things Cobbold and it was through Anthony Cobbold, keeper of the Trust, that we met. *Scattered Memories* is the product of many hours of interview and conversation with Clive and I am grateful for his assistance with this book and for helping to tease memories from the deepest recesses of my mind.

I decided to entitle the book *Scattered Memories* because that best describes what lies within its pages. Most commercially produced autobiographies are primarily concerned with the subject's career, for it is that career which justifies the writing of the book and about which the reader is most eager to learn. The writing of *Scattered Memories* has not been constrained by such concerns and has been written with a more select audience in mind. Besides, my career alone, though interesting to me, would be unlikely to keep even the most loyal reader riveted for more than a few pages. My work is one of several threads which run through the book; others include family and my love of shooting. These are the things which have provided stability and purpose through my life and which hold the story told within these pages together, providing a framework in which I relate the scattered memories of my life. Memory is a selective thing and I am sure that many of the stories I relate here will resonate with those with whom I shared them. I am also equally sure that some among my friends and family who read this book will rue the omission of their own favourite stories about me. For this, I am sorry, and can only offer the excuse that my memory now is not all it once was. Fortunately, I kept game books and logged my flights as a helicopter pilot. I hadn't looked at these books, which are full of photographs, nor at family albums for some time. They stir many happy memories and have made writing the book a great deal easier.

I am grateful to all those who have helped in bringing this book about. Particularly to Peter Wilmot-Sitwell, my brother-in-law and one of my oldest friends who has been kind enough to write the book's foreword. My cousin, Sarah Henderson, has been tremendously helpful with the opening chapter which deals with the childhood we spent together in Wiltshire during the war and in supplying the photographs, taken by her mother, of my early years. Lord Christopher Thynne, a friend since childhood, has been extremely helpful in recalling one or two amusing incidents which had slipped my mind. Alex Williams has done a wonderful job with the book's cover and I am also very grateful to Anthony Cobbold and The Cobbold Family History Trust for publishing it. Above all, I wish to thank my family. Without them *Scattered Memories* would not have been worth writing.

Nicholas Cobbold
May 2015

1. A Free Range Childhood

Like many children born in the thirties, my formative years were shaped by the war which incongruously afforded us much more freedom than children who were born either a decade earlier or a decade later. Indeed, our lives were perhaps more 'free range' than those of any generation of children before or since. Mine was particularly so. The war brought excitement to make any young boy wide-eyed and the landscape of my childhood was coloured by it. I joined army manoeuvres, rode in tanks, witnessed dogfights, saw bombs fall and even wandered amongst the wounded, trying to cheer them up. I was also convinced I had a direct role to play in the defence of my country and made plans to repel any invasion of our shores. My father and uncles were off serving king and country and I, as the 'man' of the house, would not duck my responsibilities. This absence of male authority allowed my adventurous and often mischievous nature to develop largely unchecked. I wouldn't say I was indulged by the women in my family who brought me up but I certainly got

A very early picture of me at Brantridge. (Photograph: Rosemary Crawley)

away with more than I might have if my father had been around. Discipline was not lacking altogether, though, and one woman in particular loomed large in my childhood as a benevolent dictator: my grandmother.

As I grew older, I began to understand the human cost of war from the papers, newsreels and from those I met who were fighting to defend us. Though, as children, we enjoyed more freedom, we were also required to grow up quickly. It was impossible to shield us from the horrors of war; there was a real risk that our homes might take a direct hit and we had to learn to live with the gnawing fear that those dear to us might not return from it. Like many young children, I had to come to terms with devastating personal loss, though my family was much more fortunate than many. The deaths of friends in terrible accidents unrelated to the war also impressed upon me the fragility of human life at an early age. Mine was a childhood not short in drama, excitement or tragedy. However, though it was punctuated by moments of great sadness, my overriding memories are of happy days off the leash, during which the man I was to become was shaped. I took risks, played pranks, acquired a healthy irreverence for authority and developed a love of speed. Above all, I made friends.

I was born at home in London, at 56 Rutland Gate SW7, on 5 May 1934 into a colourful family. Over the previous two centuries, the Cobbolds had done rather well for themselves. The foundation for this success was laid when Thomas Cobbold (1680-1752) moved the family's brewing business from Harwich, where the water was too brackish, to the Orwell quayside at Ipswich in 1746. The new brewery was fed by spring water from the seven

A Free Range Childhood

pools of Holy Wells where a grand family home was built. Water was channelled from the pools directly into the brewery via a narrow canal and these workings can still be seen today in Holywells Park which now belongs to the people of Ipswich. Thomas' grandson John Cobbold (1746-1835) expanded the business greatly and soon the family's wider business interests grew to encompass shipping, the railways and banking; at one time Cobbold banknotes were even issued. John married twice: his first wife, Elizabeth Wilkinson, died in 1790 having given him fifteen children; seven more followed from John's later marriage to Elizabeth Knipe (1764-1824), an energetic patron of the arts. John's descendants have since prospered in every field imaginable all over the globe.

My father, Ralph Hamilton Cobbold, was a direct descendent of John by his marriage to Elizabeth Wilkinson, though he was never in line to take the helm of the brewing business. He opted for grape rather than grain and had a successful career with the prestigious wine, liqueur and brandy merchant, Justerini & Brooks of London, ultimately becoming the company's managing director. He was a daring man, great fun and a talented sportsman. A particularly fine cricketer, he played for the Eton XI for

My father, Ralph Hamilton Cobbold.
(Photograph: Rosemary Crawley)

three years, captaining the side in 1925 before going up to Magdalene College, Cambridge where he gained his cricket Blue in 1927. He made a hundred for Eton at Lords against Harrow and 150 in a match against Winchester. Playing against the MCC in 1927, he showed his abilities as an all-rounder, making 33 runs batting at number five and took 4-81 with his accurate right arm off-breaks. He was also a fine golfer. He was a member of Royal St. George's Golf Club and played in the British Amateur Championship at Prestwick in 1934.

His father, Col. Ralph Patteson Cobbold, was a truly extraordinary man. In 1898, having resigned his commission with the 60th Rifles, he travelled widely through central Asia at a time when Great Game tensions between British India and the Russian Empire were dangerously high. Though he purported to be travelling purely for purposes of sport and recreation, it seems likely that he was spying; that an unemployed army captain was interviewed by the viceroy of India, Lord Curzon, before he set off certainly suggests that the journey had political objectives in addition to its sporting ones. Very few British travellers to the region at that time wasted the

My grandfather, Ralph Patteson Cobbold, dressed for Central Asia.

opportunity to furnish the authorities in India and in London with valuable intelligence, particularly those with a military background. Certainly the Russians thought he was a spy and he was held under house arrest in Russian Turkestan for a number of weeks, though after the exertions of his travels on the 'Roof of the World' he would later describe this detention as 'a restful holiday.' Upon his return to England he compiled a valuable report for the Intelligence Services and published a popular account of his adventures, *Innermost Asia* (1900). In the same year as his book was released he saw action in South Africa, where he served as deputy assistant adjutant-general to General John Grenfell Maxwell, military governor of Pretoria, before being invalided back to England in October. He was subsequently mentioned in despatches.

Shortly afterwards he was selected by St. John Brodrick, secretary of state for war and the Marquess of Lansdowne, foreign secretary, for a delicate mission to Abyssinia to help co-ordinate the operations of the Emperor Menelik II's army with those of Britain and Italy against the marauding Mad Mullah. He went twice to Abyssinia and was interviewed by King Edward VII both before his first mission and after his last. Upon his return from the second of these missions in 1903, he was introduced to Minnie Diana Pitt, a daughter of the great family of English politicians and widow of the South African diamond magnate, Hermann Eckstein, who, in partnership with Alfred Beit and Sir Julius Wernher formed the Central Mining Group. Minnie became my grandfather's second wife (of three) in 1905. My father was born to the couple in 1906, my grandfather's only child.

In the summer of 1914, my grandfather was in Canada,

possibly on business. During his stay he journeyed to Kirkland Lake in Northern Ontario. There he met a man named Harry Oakes, a gold prospector. The land surrounding the lake was crowded with fortune hunters, but Oakes considered they were digging in the wrong place and that greater riches lay beneath the lake itself. Oakes lamented that he could not afford to drain the lake to prove his theory and it seems that my grandfather offered Oakes an investment in return for a substantial share of any future profits. A deal was struck and my grandfather made his way back to civilisation in order to arrange the finance. It was then that he learned that Britain had declared war on Germany and, ever patriotic, he decided to head back to England rather than invest in Oakes' scheme. In so doing, he turned his back on an opportunity which would have brought him (and his descendants) unimaginable wealth. When the lake was eventually drained, Oakes' Lakeshore Goldmine became one of the richest in the world, making Oakes, himself, Canada's wealthiest man. Having made his millions, Oakes later retired to the Bahamas where, in 1943, he was brutally murdered in mysterious circumstances.

When he returned home, my grandfather signed up with the 1st Ox and Bucks Light Infantry with the rank of captain. At the age of forty-seven he led his men on the first day of the Battle of the Somme. His battalion remained there for the entire course of the appalling battle, enduring heavy losses. He later served at Béthune. Nothing if not durable, he survived the Great War, serving with distinction; he was mentioned in despatches for a second time and won a DSO, before finally hanging up his sword with the rank of colonel. I recall meeting this remarkable

A Free Range Childhood

character, a true *Boy's Own* hero, not very often, though I do remember, as a child, visiting his home, Penrice, in Cornwall. I also went to visit him in hospital in London towards the end of his life.

My mother, (Norah) Veronica (Vandeleur) Christie-Miller also came from a family of note. Her father's family, the Christie-Millers were Edinburgh landowners; her mother's, the Vandeleurs, owned a large chunk of County Clare around the town of Kilrush and had their own proud tradition of military service. Lieutenant-Colonel Seymour Vandeleur DSO, Scots Guards and Irish Guards, my great uncle, was a fearless, decorated soldier who served all over Africa in the late nineteenth century. He saw action in Uganda, Nigeria, Egypt and, in 1898, with Kitchener's army in the Sudan at the Battle of Omdurman. He met a dramatic and heroic death in South Africa in 1901. The locomotive he was travelling on to take up a command at Nylstroom,

My mother, Veronica Christie-Miller.
(Photograph: Rosemary Crawley)

north of Pretoria, was blown from the tracks by a notorious Irish train-wrecker, Jack Hindon. In the immediate aftermath of the explosion, fifty or so Boers opened fire on the beleaguered train's passenger carriages. Two ladies travelling in Seymour's carriage were wounded and he instructed the civilian passengers to lie on the floor. As he opened the door to assume command of the other soldiers travelling on the train, he was immediately confronted by a Boer, named Uys, who shot him dead at point blank range. Seymour's extraordinary career was later documented in a eulogistic book by his great friend, the renowned general, Sir (Frederick) Ivor Maxse. Seymour had been Maxse's best man.

The Christie-Millers and the Vandeleurs came together in 1904 when Sydney Richardson Christie-Miller and (Evelyn) Norah Vandeleur, my grandparents, married. A year later, my mother was born, the eldest of five. She was raised at Britwell Court, near Slough, a property which had been in the Christie-Miller family for some years and which my grandfather inherited in 1903. Britwell Court boasted one of the finest private libraries in the world, housing the considerable collection of William Henry Miller, one of my grandfather's forebears, who had first bought the house for the family in 1830. No fewer than three full-time librarians were employed to look after the collection which contained hundreds of extremely valuable first editions. After the First World War, my grandfather became concerned by the relentless encroachment of nearby Slough which was sprawling ever nearer to the estate and he sold Britwell in 1919. At the same time he began the process of dispersing the contents of its library, placing the collection in the hands of Sotheby's, who sold the collection in lots. Ten annual sales were held, ultimately realising

A Free Range Childhood

a sum of £643,000, a full quarter of a million pounds more than any other collection, British or American, had ever yielded before. Among the 'star' items, a copy of the Mazarin bible went for £21,000 and a fourth edition (1599) of Shakespeare's *Venus and Adonis* fetched £15,100. From Britwell, the family moved to the magnificent Clarendon Park estate, just east of Salisbury, a place which would play a great part in my childhood and which would become very dear to me.

My mother was a dashing woman in her youth and very independent. In the early thirties, before she married my father in 1933, she took flying lessons, something very unusual for a woman in those days. Her instructor was Geordie Ward, youngest son of the Earl of Dudley, who went on to fly in the war as a group captain and who, later, served as secretary of state for air in Harold Macmillan's government. Sadly, my mother's exciting hobby was short-lived and came to an end when a photograph appeared in *The Tatler* of her having a lesson at Heston Airport. When her parents saw the picture, a fearful row ensued and they insisted she stop. She also loved driving and once, wanting to be independent, bought herself a Bentley so that she could get to Scotland for a holiday. It seems I inherited my love of speed from her.

I recall very little of my early years spent in London but have vague recollections of summer holidays spent with my uncles, aunts and cousins at Brantridge Park, a large country estate near Balcombe, West Sussex. My family would take the house, once a favourite retreat of Queen Victoria, for some weeks each summer and I remember lying in my pram there, aged two or three, and seeing the sunlight streak through its silver tassels.

Brantridge had ninety acres and a swimming pool. Photographs I have since seen of these holidays depict a sunny pre-war idyll and exude a sense of great family fun.

I was five years old when war broke out. Our home in London was no safe place for children and, like many, I was evacuated to the comparative safety of the countryside along with my infant twin sisters, Clare and Anne with whom I have always been very close, who were not quite a year old. Evacuation for us was far more comfortable than for the majority of children who were wrenched from their families to live in cramped conditions with complete strangers away from Britain's major cities. We spent the war surrounded by our family in the idyllic surroundings of Clarendon Park. The estate was now in the capable hands of my grandmother, Norah, my grandfather having died in 1931. She was an indomitable woman and, as soon as war broke out, she insisted that her three daughters - my mother, Rosemary Crawley and Lavender Sykes - and their children should see out hostilities in the relative safety of Clarendon. My sisters and I, Rosemary's three daughters (a fourth would arrive during the war) and Lavender's four all moved into Clarendon where we were looked after by a small army of nannies and my grandmother's staff. I later learned that my grandmother was not the only one to offer us sanctuary. Our parents received an offer that, if accepted, would have removed us even further from danger. Bob Coe, an anglophile American diplomat who had been to Magdalen College, Oxford, was a great friend of the family. He offered to take all of us and the children of his other friends, Lord Weymouth and Lord Stavordale, to his Wyoming home for the duration of the war. It was an extraordinarily

A Free Range Childhood

generous offer from a man whom we all adored but, individually, all our parents declined the offer. It was to be at Clarendon and not Wyoming that we would spend the war. When we arrived in Wiltshire in 1939, my two uncles, Sammy and Michael Christie-Miller, the latter just twelve years my senior and much more like an older brother to me, were also living at Clarendon. Both soon went off to war: only one would survive it.

My uncle, Michael Christie-Miller and my grandmother, Norah. Each played a large part in my childhood. (Photograph: Rosemary Crawley)

Clarendon comprised a grand house with extremely large rooms, onto which a more functional three storey Victorian wing had been attached. This wing became home. The middle and upper floors housed the nurseries in which we slept and ate: the middle floor also had what was known as the bachelors' wing where unmarried guests would stay, while the kitchens, laundry and servants' quarters were on the ground floor. The wing was served by two hand-operated unmanned lifts or 'dumbwaiters', one for conveying food, the other, much larger, for carrying luggage. There were separate nurseries for each family, the Cobbolds, the Crawleys and the Sykes, and each had its own nanny who was helped by nursery maids and a footman.

The Cobbolds and the Crawleys at Clarendon in 1941.
Back row: My father, my mother, my sister Anne and my uncle, Cosmo Crawley.
Front row: My sister Clare, me, my cousins, Henrietta, Sarah and Camilla Crawley.
(Photograph: Rosemary Crawley)

Our nanny, Nanny Keeling, had been with us at Rutland Gate and, while at Clarendon, she fell in love with and married my grandmother's head gardener, a man named Jim Mouland. As young children, all our meals were taken in the nursery. We never ate downstairs with the adults, though Sarah Crawley, my eldest cousin, and I would sometimes look in on them having breakfast on our way out for the day. Occasionally, particularly if male guests were staying, we would perform a trick. Sarah would throw butter pats in my direction and I would catch them in my mouth, to great applause. When I was older and had my own room I was allowed to join the adults for breakfast, though my grandmother was never present, always taking breakfast in bed. Later still, after I had started at Eton, I was allowed to go down for dinner.

Clarendon's coal-fired central heating system was seldom turned on, fuel being in short supply, and the house was often cold, being heated mainly by fires. Granny, as we would always call her, would often stand with her back to a fire, hitch up her skirt at the back revealing voluminous long beige bloomers and warm her bottom. She thought nobody knew she did this, but Sarah and I would spy on her, giggling. Only two rooms downstairs in the main house were in daily use, the dining room and the smoking room. The library was occasionally used for more formal gatherings. Granny used to hold knitting bees there, inviting local ladies round to knit in support of the Personal Service League. The fruits of their efforts, usually red or green sweaters, would be sent off to clothe children in the slums, though I do remember that we children wore them too. Sarah and I once sabotaged one of these charitable gatherings by unravelling a ball of wool and creating a huge cat's cradle across the doorway to the library. We crept out beneath it, leaving Granny and her ladies trapped. When they eventually escaped, Granny came looking for us and we got into terrible trouble. The drawing room was only ever used to stage the lavish children's Christmas parties which Granny put on for us, our friends and the other children on the estate. She would transform the room into a wonderland, lining the walls with Wendy houses, covered in gold paper, which were shops from which we would buy presents with chocolate money. On these occasions Clarendon's grand hall also became a playground. We would slide down the bannisters of its magnificent double staircase, landing softly on a large mattress which had been placed atop a long trestle table. This was not for the faint-hearted and on one occasion I sustained a painful injury - a rather large splinter in my bottom. Of course, such antics were seldom allowed indoors. Besides, who would want to play inside when the estate boasted five thousand acres? This was my playground.

We wanted for little at Clarendon. The estate provided delicacies that most could only dream of during the war. Rabbits were always in plentiful supply and our cooks would strip the backs off them, beat them and cover them in breadcrumbs so that they resembled Wiener schnitzel. We also ate game and venison and the kitchen garden provided us with vegetables. We weren't entirely self-sufficient and a car went to Salisbury once a week to collect rations for the estate. With rationing hitting people hard, Sarah and I recognised an opportunity to make some extra pocket money. We each had a pet rabbit, which did what rabbits do, and we would take their babies to Salisbury market and sell them for food for sixpence each. I was more successful in this venture than Sarah, whose rabbit, Janet, had a tendency to eat her own young.

Tantalising delicacies would occasionally arrive at Clarendon from America in the form of food parcels intended for the family and for those billeted nearby. Prior to collection, these would be stored in the skylight room between the main house and the Victorian wing. Within these parcels were canned foods, Lucky Strike cigarettes and, of greatest appeal to us, Hershey chocolate bars, almost impossible to resist. Every so often, Sarah and I would sneak into the skylight room, deftly open one of the parcels and take just one Hershey Bar which we would later break in two and share. These daring missions came to an abrupt end one day when Granny came into the room for something and caught us red-handed.

    Sarah was just sixteen months older than me and we became inseparable, more like brother and sister than cousins. During the early years of the war, my sisters and younger cousins were too young to be allowed out to play on their own but Sarah and I were more or less given the run of the estate. We would spend all day outside, whatever the weather, rambling, riding and cycling around the grounds. Beyond the well-tended formal gardens and large, walled kitchen garden lay a rolling landscape in which we lost ourselves. Sarah was particularly keen on riding and she would regularly saddle and bridle both our ponies, mine was called *Daisy*, hers *Merrylegs*, and lead them round to the front door from where we would ride off together. I was less keen on riding than her and this was her way of ensuring I joined her. A favourite route took us through a narrow path in the woods and I perfected the trick of grabbing a low hanging branch while Sarah led *Daisy* on. Sarah would then double back with *Daisy* and I would drop back into the saddle. We were usually out all day. At lunchtime the odd job man would attempt to get our attention by standing outside the house and ringing a large bell. We were often out of earshot and would sometimes go without lunch. On other occasions we would take a picnic and, if it rained, we would tether our ponies next to each other, drape a groundsheet across their backs and munch sandwiches underneath.

Sarah and I enjoying the freedom of Clarendon with *Daisy* and *Merrylegs*. (Photograph: Rosemary Crawley)

The estate, though very large, was not crossed by a single public road and was therefore very safe; three drives led to the house, two of which, the Salisbury and Pitton drives were each two miles long; the other, perhaps half a mile long led to the village of Alderbury. Despite having such a vast area in which to play, we would sometimes venture beyond the confines of the estate's boundaries where other temptations lay. We would, for example, risk crossing the busy Salisbury to Southampton road (A36) on horseback or by bicycle to pay a visit to Mrs Safe's sweetshop which was close to the gates at the end of the Salisbury drive. These expeditions usually proved disappointing. Our nannies held our coupons for sweets and cashed them in on our behalf at the village shop in nearby Alderbury and we would only ever walk out of the Mrs Safe's shop with two Liquorice Allsorts each. We didn't like them – but neither did anyone else and this probably explained her readiness to part with them free of charge.

We were not Clarendon's only evacuees. Shortly after hostilities commenced, my grandmother generously offered a haven for the pupils of Solent Road School in Portsmouth, a city that would be a sure target for German bombers. Children and staff from the school were housed in Clarendon's stable block which was hastily adapted for the purpose and lessons continued. The stables were also the fitting location for the nativity plays which the school used to stage each year and which we used to look forward to with great excitement. For almost the entire war, there were about a hundred people living in the house and the stables, including the school children and a number of paying guests. In addition the estate was populated by a number of tenant farmers. My grandmother was a magnificent organiser and personally ensured that the estate ran smoothly, ruling with an iron rod. She was uncompromising in her standards and almost everyone, including her daughters, lived in fear of falling below them: only her grandchildren were afforded any slack.

Sarah, ever a tom boy, and I would often play with the boys from the school who were of a similar age. Their ringleader was called 'Kipper', who was a little older than me, perhaps the same age as Sarah. Once, I couldn't have been more than about six or seven, Kipper, a few of his gang, Sarah and I were playing towards the bottom of the Pitton drive where there were some very tall fir trees. We all started to climb and, determined not to be outdone by a girl, I raced up my tree, climbing beyond the height Sarah was able to reach on hers. Perhaps in my haste, I hadn't realised how far up I was, but I suddenly froze. Climbing down from a tree is usually a more precarious business than climbing up one and I was well and truly stuck and quite frightened. We were about a mile and a half from the house with no adult in sight to help. As Sarah was shouting at me, telling me not to be so silly, Kipper calmly volunteered to run off in search of help. He made for one of the farms on the estate, Piper's, which was much closer than the main house and he soon returned with a couple of burly farmhands who managed to help me down. Though shaken, the experience did not stifle my sense of adventure or instil in me a fear of heights.

I learned to shoot at Clarendon. From about eight years old, I had a single-barrelled hammer 410 shotgun and an air gun and the estate's keepers taught me how to handle it, taking me out to shoot pigeons, pheasants and rabbits. As I became more confident with the gun nothing was safe from my improving aim, including Granny's chickens. These were very dear to her and every day she would collect their eggs in a basket, though she delegated the less rewarding task of feeding them to her staff. When I was about nine or ten, I contracted measles. I was removed from the nursery and quarantined in a large bedroom, No. 1, in a corner of the main house. A sheet was doused in disinfectant and draped over the doorway to contain my germs. Confined and terribly bored, I persuaded Sarah to smuggle in my air gun and some pellets and then gave her further instructions.

A Free Range Childhood

A few minutes later, I heard the clucking of Granny's chickens beneath my window, Sarah having driven them there. I went to the window, took aim, and fired, pranging a few before stowing the gun and slipping back into bed to resume the pose of a sick boy. Granny was incensed – at Sarah who was unable to drive the survivors away quickly enough and was caught red-handed with dead and injured poultry lying at her feet. I escaped the incident blame free.

With my airgun I thought it great fun taking aim at the boxed windows at ground level around the house which gave light to the basement. Regular discoveries of broken panes caused bewilderment among the household: I never owned up to this vandalism and I was never caught. More structured training in the use of firearms came in the form of organised shoots at Clarendon which my grandmother regularly put on for army officers billeted in the area. Sarah and I were allowed to drive the game cart which was great fun. We were chased by a bull once and galloped across a field to escape with partridges flying off in

In charge of the game cart with Sarah. The horse is *Barney*. (Photograph: Rosemary Crawley)

all directions. These shoots were enormous fun and I felt very grown up: my lifelong love of the sport had taken root.

At about the same time as I learned to shoot, I also learned how to drive. My uncle, Michael, taught me in his own car, an old 'Rattletrap', while he was home on leave. I don't think I was allowed to drive unsupervised for some time and doubt I would have been able to reach the pedals. Not that I was much of a hazard to other motorists, my early experience at the wheel being gained on Clarendon's deserted, long private drives. Of course this was enormous fun for a young boy and it caused great annoyance to Sarah, who, being a girl, was not allowed to drive even though she was older than me. The early experience I gained behind the wheel stood me in good stead when I was older: when I came to take my test I had already been driving for nine years and I passed a day after my seventeenth birthday.

Though we had been removed to Clarendon to escape the war, its location ensured that we were never far from military activity. Southern Command was just a few miles away at Wilton; Southampton and Portsmouth were close as were the airfields of Boscombe Down and Old Sarum. From the estate, we could see barrage balloons swaying over Southampton and, at night, search lights trying to pick out German bombers. The Battle of Britain was waged overhead and I became fascinated with aeroplanes. I was given a copy of Jane's *All the World's Aircraft* and could soon identify every aircraft on each side, including Japanese planes, though of course I never saw one in the skies. At Boscombe Down in 1942, I saw the first Flying Fortress to arrive in Britain and was allowed to climb all over it. I also saw the early trials for the Mosquito. On another occasion, one of my uncles took me to

Portsmouth to see the construction of an extraordinary piece of engineering, something he claimed would alter the course of the war. I was too young to understand (or perhaps be told) that I was witnessing the construction of sections of the huge, artificial Mulberry Harbour, which would be towed into position off the Normandy coast at Arromanches on D-Day to support the Allied advance through northern France.

In addition to the comings and goings of military units in the area, Clarendon saw plenty of its own war drama, particularly during the Battle of Britain. The natural instincts of a young boy were to rush out on to the lawns and gaze skywards at the action taking place overhead. For as long as I could, before my grandmother would quickly shoo me back into the safety of the house, I would stand transfixed, my neck craned to watch dogfights between Messerschmitts and Spitfires. One of the latter actually crashed into woods on the estate, minus its pilot who had presumably bailed out. I remember walking around the wreck, fascinated, before it was removed by the authorities. On another occasion the helmet and goggles of a German flier fell through the skylight room; the fate of their owner or his plane was never known to us. Bombs fell on the estate on at least six occasions as German bombers emptied their loads before heading home. We suspected that Clarendon, a large English country house, was being deliberately targeted. Its large cellar was converted into an air raid shelter into which we would move when there was a heightened risk of bombing during the Blitz. The ceiling of the cellar was bolstered by large wooden props, cut by the estate's carpenters, to protect it from falling in in the event of a direct hit on the house. Still, I would only take cover when called in by my grandmother, fascinated by the goings on in the skies. Once, I was standing on the lawns with Mouland, the head gardener, when we saw a German plane drop a bomb not far from us. We watched the bomb plummet towards the ground, perhaps a mile away. Though we couldn't see the impact because of the lay of the land, it was clear that the property of a family we knew had taken a direct hit. We later learned that, thankfully, the family had been out when their house was struck. The only person in it at the time had been the daily, who, by enormous good fortune, had happened to be turning a mattress at the precise moment the bomb exploded. Miraculously, the mattress absorbed the blast and protected the maid from shrapnel. She survived almost without a scratch.

Prior to the successes of D-Day, the possibility of a German invasion of southern England loomed large. This prospect did not escape me, despite my tender years, and I made thorough preparations to thwart the Wehrmacht should it ever reach the gates of Clarendon. I intended to conduct a single-handed guerrilla campaign against the invaders and made all manner of preparations to repel Hitler's finest. As the Germans approached Clarendon, I would evacuate to my command centre – one of several dens Sarah and I had made in the woods on the estate. This particular hideout was equipped with a stove and was protected by an early warning system, comprising a tripwire which would cause a bell to fall from a tree, sounding the alarm. I had pinched the bell from one of the hall porters. I dug a tunnel connecting my hideout with another tunnel which was built by troops to act as an air raid shelter for the school. The entrance to the shelter was some distance away from my den enabling me to get in and out undetected. My plan was to fend off the enemy with my single-barrelled 410. Should I need to dig in against a tenacious enemy, I had buried cartridges and food supplies in the woods surrounding my headquarters. Among the food which would sustain me should I become besieged were hard-to-get 'delicacies' such as spam, which I was given by American soldiers who came to visit. My friends and family were aware of the den's existence but thought it just like any other which a boy of my age might construct and play in. I kept its military function secret, perhaps in fear that its role as a key link in the nation's defences might be compromised by loose talk within the household. After the war, my uncle Sammy, who returned from fighting in the Middle East, destroyed the den which, anyway, had become neglected as I spent more time at school and less at Clarendon. As the eldest son, Sammy later inherited the house after my grandmother's death in 1966. Michael, his younger brother, whom I idolised, did not return from the war. Serving with the 4th Coldstream, he was killed when his tank took a direct hit in the Calvados region of Normandy on 30 July 1944. He was just twenty-two years old. I was ten and he had always been like an older brother to me.

    I think I remember seeing the postman cycle up the drive holding the yellow telegram which bore the terrible news. I was distraught. An air of gloom descended over Clarendon and my cousins and I were sent away to Birse Castle in Aberdeenshire to escape it. Birse was owned by a dear family friend, Lord Cowdray, and had been taken for the summer months by members of my family. We were joined there by friends and stayed for a fortnight though the diversion did little to ease the pain I felt at losing Michael. Some sixty years later, I went to Normandy to visit his grave. Before I went, I rang the Coldstream Guards to ask for the precise location of Michael's grave. The information I received turned out to be wrong and I went to three war cemeteries in search of his headstone. When I eventually walked through the gates of the actual cemetery, I instinctively knew exactly where the grave was and went straight to it. I miss Michael to this day and I still wear a pair of his slippers, embroidered with his initials.

I saw little of my father during the war. He, and a number of his friends, joined up several months prior to its outbreak, anticipating the failure of diplomatic efforts to avert hostilities. His training was complete by September 1939 when war was declared and he was ready for service. He had joined the 1st Coldstream and was initially deployed in the defence of the south coast before becoming an instructor at Sandhurst. In June 1944, he followed on behind the D-Day landings, fought through France and reached Germany as Nazi resistance crumpled. He ended the war with the rank of major. He was among the first into Rheims where he was warmly welcomed by his old friends from the wine trade. In April 1945 he liberated Stalag XI-B, a prisoner of war camp in Lower Saxony. When he walked through the gates he was met with a guard of honour, organised by RSM John Clifford Lord of the 1st Parachute Brigade. My father was greatly impressed by Lord, formerly a Grenadier Guardsman, whom he described as 'a majestic figure....with gleaming brass, immaculate webbing, razor-edged trouser creases, dazzling boots [and] a spectacular salute.' Lord was a remarkable leader and organiser who refused the offer of a transfer to a more comfortable NCO

A Free Range Childhood

camp in order to remain with his men; for his outstanding leadership in Stalag XI-B he was awarded the MBE.

My father (left) ready for Pirbright with his friend, John Fox-Strangways and his brother-in-law, Cosmo Crawley. (Photograph: Rosemary Crawley)

My mother was also often absent from Clarendon. She 'did her bit', taking a number of driving jobs to support the war effort. As I recall, this involved a stint with the Red Cross and she also worked as a librarian. My father's duties took him all over the south of England and my mother would sometimes join him. I remember them taking houses together at Longbridge Deverill and at Midsomer Norton. I would sometimes join them, but they never stayed in one place for long. Certainly, Clarendon was the place I called home for the duration of the war.

I must have been about ten years old when my father, then an instructor at Sandhurst, called me out on an exercise. In flagrant breach of army regulations, for three days I sat in the front gunner's compartment of a Sherman tank, wearing a regimental beret, much too big for me, which was pulled down over my face to disguise my youth. Later, just before D-Day, the whole of the Guards Armoured Brigade, including the Coldstream Guards, my father's old battalion was stationed at Clarendon. The estate's Salisbury and Pitton drives, each two miles long, had tanks parked every twenty yards. With D-Day approaching, secrecy was paramount and the drives were lined with trees affording the

With my Crawley cousins on board a tank on one of Clarendon's drives.
(Photograph: Rosemary Crawley)

tanks cover from any German reconnaissance planes. It was quite a sight and Sarah and I climbed in and out of the tanks and took 'brew ups' with the men. We were also given lifts up and down these lines on army motorcycles. Helmets were not deemed necessary. It was all very exciting and we were largely oblivious to the great dangers these soldiers were about to confront. Many of them must have paid the ultimate sacrifice on the beaches of Normandy or in the hinterland beyond. Remarkably, all of the officers in my father's company, all of whom I knew well, survived.

We would often have friends to stay at Clarendon and these visits were reciprocated. Every summer during my childhood from about the age of seven, I would spend a week or ten days at Longleat with the Thynne family, sometimes accompanied by Sarah. Petrol was in short supply, so we took the train. Someone from Clarendon would take us to the railway station at Salisbury and then someone from Longleat would collect us at the other end at Warminster. Christopher Thynne was the same age as me and a great friend. We would also play with his older brother, Alexander, who was Sarah's age and Caroline who was four years older than any of us and quite stunning. Indeed, the Thynnes, parents and children, were all incredibly good-looking, without doubt the best-looking family I have ever seen. Caroline would later marry the Duke of Beaufort. We didn't stay at Longleat House but just down the road at Sturford Mead, a much more modest, though still very comfortable house, the home of their parents, Lord and Lady Weymouth. Lord Weymouth was seldom there, away serving with the Royal Wiltshire Yeomanry.

During the war, the 5th Marquess of Bath, the children's grandfather, had given much of his home over to the US Army for use as a hospital. Consequently, there was a steady flow of military traffic to and from Longleat House. Often, from Sturford Mead, we would walk the short distance to the gates of the estate to watch American jeeps and trucks turning in. We soon discovered that we could employ Caroline's obvious charms to persuade some of the GIs to part with their rations. The rest of us would hide out of sight while Caroline would sit on the gate, legs dangling and looking gorgeous and, sure enough, chocolate bars and cigarettes would come her way in good numbers. We younger ones would greedily enjoy the chocolate, Milky Bars in the main, while Caroline would pocket the cigarettes. This tobacco haul was added to from the main house. Old Lord Bath lived in rooms in one corner of the house, almost as a recluse, though he didn't mind our visits at all. He was completely oblivious to the fact that while one of us was talking to him, another would be pinching his cigarettes.

The army hospital was not out of bounds to us. Christopher and I would sometimes wander through its 'wards' and would chat to the men, many of whom had horrific injuries. Contrary to the customary practice of visitors bringing treats for patients, it was we who benefited from these visits as, cheered up by our presence, the wounded GIs would offer us chocolate and 'candy' from their rations. Thanks to the presence of American soldiers in and around our homes we did better than most for confectionery.

Strangely, despite having acre upon acre in which to play at Longleat, we liked nothing more than to venture up on to the

A Free Range Childhood

roof of the house. There, more than fifty feet up and with no safety rails, we would play football and jump between parts of the building, knowing that a mistimed leap would result in serious injury or, more likely, death. Sarah, plucky as ever, would join us and would often play in goal, a particularly perilous position in our lofty games of football. Not all was innocent fun atop the roofs of Longleat. Lord Bath's housekeeper, Mrs Parker, was a fearsome woman with exacting standards which,

The roof of Longleat House. An unlikely football pitch. (Photograph: Alison Churchill courtesy of Mendip Cave Registry & Archive)

sometimes, our antics upset. I remember her clothes, from top to bottom, being so stiffly starched that one could hear her coming from some distance. She had the habit of keeping a fire going in her room all day so that she could make herself a cup of tea whenever she had a break. Christopher and I worked out which of the roof's many chimneys served Mrs Parker's room and thought it great fun to extinguish her fire with water. On one occasion, we didn't just pour water down the chimney; we lobbed in full glass bottles which must have made an awful mess upon impact. We could only imagine the rage that this would induce in Mrs Parker whenever she returned to her room to find steam in her grate and shattered glass all around her room because we were never brought to book.

I vividly remember one particularly bizarre incident which occurred at Jobs Mill home of the 6th Lord Bath (formerly Viscount Weymouth), Christopher's father, on the Longleat estate (he never lived in Longleat House). I must have been about sixteen or seventeen and Lord Bath, had invited me to quite a grand dinner. About halfway through the meal he instructed his butler to bring another bottle of champagne. The butler, Donald, returned some moments later and informed Lord Bath that he was unable to retrieve a bottle. When asked why by his master, Donald replied, 'Because there's a naked lady in the refrigerator, my Lord.' Christopher and I were understandably thrilled when Lord Bath asked us to investigate and we rushed off to the kitchens. Sure enough, one of Lord Bath's guests, a lady named Mavis Wheeler, had stripped off and was trying to shut herself in the refrigerator, presumably to cool down. Mavis lived a colourful life. She was the widow of the famous prankster Horace de Vere Cole and had later married the archaeologist Sir Mortimer Wheeler who divorced her in 1942. In 1954, she ended up in a different kind of cooler (prison) when she shot and wounded her lover, Lord Vivian, a brother-in-law of Lord Bath. The couple had had a blazing drunken row in a pub and Mavis had stormed off home. When Vivian followed some time later, he found himself locked out and had to prise open a window to get in. As soon as he had climbed through, he was confronted by Mavis who was waving his old army pistol. She steadied herself, took aim, and shot him in the balls.

At Clarendon, my grandmother kept an open house and there were always guests coming and going, often to shoot. She also took in paying guests and one such was Lord Carnarvon, who, being too old to fight, had taken a desk job with the army in Salisbury. Rather than commute to Salisbury from his Berkshire home, Highclere Castle (best known as Downton Abbey in the popular television series), Lord Carnarvon would stay with us at Clarendon for long periods, occupying bedroom No. 3 in the main house. He made a great fuss of us 'dear children.' He was extremely generous and was the first person ever to give me a £5 note, in those days a large white flimsy piece of paper, as a tip when I was just about to return to school after the holidays. He would sometimes line us all up in order of height and produce a jar of expensive sweets from the famous London chocolatier, Charbonnel et Walker, before popping one into our mouths.

Clarendon.

As well as with the Thynnes, we played with the children and grandchildren of my grandmother's and my parents' friends who lived in houses nearby. Among these were the Radnors of

Longford Castle, the Fox-Strangways of Melbury and the Morrisons of Fonthill. On visits to Fonthill, Sarah and I would race tricycles up and down its passageways with James and Charles Morrison. The Morrison boys were both older than me and were strapping Scots lads who gave no quarter and enjoyed a bit of rough and tumble – Sarah and I enjoyed playing with them but we would often return with a few bruises. Of course, these friends were regular visitors to Clarendon too, while others came from a broad range of society. Generals from Southern Command at Wilton visited regularly, as did the Bishop of Salisbury and the socialites Cecil Beaton and David Herbert who were great friends of my grandmother. Once, when the bishop was visiting, Sarah and I played a trick on Granny. Earlier, some American soldiers whom I had befriended had given me something I had never even heard of before - a whoopee cushion. It didn't take me long to hatch a plan to deploy it to maximum effect. Dinner at Clarendon was always a grand affair and Granny always sat at the head of the table. Conveniently, her Chippendale dining chair was the only one of the twenty-four around the grand table that always had a cushion on it. On this particular evening it would have two. Long before the guests arrived, I primed the device between chair and cushion and waited for events to unfold. Sarah and I were not going to miss this, and as the guests walked through to dinner we were hiding behind the screen from where the servants brought out the food. All stood as the bishop said grace. Then, as everyone sat down to eat, the sound of an enormous ripping fart, coming from Granny's direction, reverberated around the room. None of the guests knew where to look. Of course, in those days of heightened social decorum, no one knew what a whoopee cushion was and so no one, at first, suspected that a childish prank had been played until our howls of laughter from the corner of the room gave the game away and the device was discovered. Still sniggering, Sarah and I sloped off somewhere where we laughed uncontrollably for some time. After their initial shock, I think Granny and her guests saw the funny side of our trick.

I went to prep school quite late and had very little structured education beforehand. My grandmother's own efforts to educate Sarah and me were short-lived. One day, she summoned us to the smoking room where she cleared a long table and told us to sit down. She announced that she was going to give us a History lesson and opened *Our Island Story*, an illustrated history of Britain from the Romans up until the death of Queen Victoria. She couldn't have got much further than about a quarter of the way through one story when she declared that she was bored and snapped the book shut. That was that. Not long afterwards, I began Latin lessons with a tutor, Mr McCann, who came to Clarendon from Salisbury two or three days a week. I can't say I enjoyed these much as they kept me from my adventures outdoors.

Aged nine, my parents sent me to Ludgrove School, near Wokingham. There, I was surrounded by many of the friends I had grown up with, including Christopher Thynne and another of my great childhood friends, Giles Fox-Strangways, eldest son of Lord Stavordale. We all started Ludgrove on the same day and it seemed I would be very happy there. As things turned out, I stayed just two terms before my parents removed me without explanation. When I was older, they told me they had been concerned about the education the school offered and, that of twelve boys who went to Eton from the school during my short time there, eleven had taken the lowest form possible. Today, they wouldn't even have got in. The school's masters were, they maintained, either too young and about to join the forces or too old. In the mould of Victorian private schools, Ludgrove, at that time, placed greater emphasis on achievements on the playing

Ludgrove School where I was very happy – briefly. I would later send my son there. (Photograph: Jon Combe)

field than in the classroom. This ethos was firmly entrenched and was upheld by its long serving headmaster, Alan Barber, a former captain of Yorkshire.

My parents had put me down for Eton at birth and, disillusioned with Ludgrove, they approached Jack Peterson, my intended tutor at Eton, and asked him which school would give me the best grounding, academically. He suggested St Peter's Court at Broadstairs, a small school with an excellent academic

A Free Range Childhood

record which had been attended by two of George V's sons. Shortly after the outbreak of war, the school was evacuated to Devon, to a large country house, Shobrooke Park Mansion, near Crediton, which was owned by Sir John Frederick Shelley, vice-chairman of Devon County Council. It was here that I arrived, barely ten years old, having been wrenched away from my friends. When I was much older, my father would apologise for removing me from Ludgrove.

St Peter's Court was not renowned for producing sportsmen and there were few sporting facilities at its temporary home at Shobrooke, although I remember a makeshift football pitch in the grounds. The war also deprived me of any coaching I undoubtedly would have received from my father, an extremely talented sportsman, who was occupied with his regiment. At an age when most boys are being taught the forward defensive or the cover drive, I had no one to coach me. At home I was surrounded by women and, now, I was at a school which considered sport much less important than scholarly pursuits. I was immediately unhappy at Shobrooke even though I could hold my own academically. Occasional moments of levity would bring a smile to my face. During a lesson on the Napoleonic Wars, a master asked us to name three of Bonaparte's marshals: one boy quickly shouted out, 'Marshal Ney, Marshal Soult and Marshall Snelgrove.' Such incidents lifted my mood only briefly but, as fate would have it, I was not to remain at Shobrooke long.

At about 4 o'clock in the morning on Tuesday 23 January 1945, an icily cold night, I was tucked up in bed in my dormitory. Suddenly, I was awoken as a boy returned from the lavatory. To our great alarm, behind him were great clouds of billowing smoke. We were on the upper floor in a corner of the house and I sensed straight away that things did not look very good. Our dormitory captain told the dozen or so of us in the room to remain in our beds, but I instinctively knew that we must escape as quickly as we could. We opened the door of the dormitory, intending to take the quickest route out of the building, down the grand double staircase in the middle of the house to the hallway. We crept low to the ground to avoid inhaling smoke but on reaching the staircase it became clear very quickly that this route was impossible. The hallway, which was the full height of the house, was filled with acrid black smoke and molten glass from its domed roof was falling onto the stairs. There was nothing for it but to turn around and to try to make our escape through one of the upstairs windows. The best route left available to us was through a window which was directly above the roof of a portico under which carriages would be driven to drop guests at the front door during the house's Victorian heyday. We quickly stripped our beds and tied sheets together to make ropes down which we could climb to safety. Jumping, even from the roof of the portico would most likely have incurred injury, for though Shobrooke had only two storeys, its ceilings were very high.

Despite the predicament of our situation, I remember being struck at how orderly the evacuation was. Almost without exception there was no panic; boys remained polite and waited patiently for their turn to descend, helping those either side of them. The youngest boys were just seven years old. It was the first time I noticed the great capacity of people to behave well under extreme pressure which I have seen on a number of occasions since. The calm which prevailed no doubt saved many lives. I was not aware of the presence of any staff to help us with our escape though later reports in the local press listed three members of staff who had fractured limbs and one who had sustained spinal injuries; the school's headmaster would later tell the inquest that he had assisted boys onto the portico but I don't remember him being there at all. One by one we clambered out of the window and onto the portico before lowering ourselves hand over hand using the makeshift ropes. My sheet-ladder broke as I was halfway down and I fell onto the door scraper beside the portico. With adrenaline flowing, I felt nothing at the time, but later discovered I had a very nasty bruise. I am not sure whether I had bothered to put on my dressing gown and slippers before escaping. If I had been wearing slippers they must have fallen off during my descent for I remember the cold as my bare feet sank into the several inches of snow which lay on the ground. The sensation was strange as the rest of my body remained hot from being so close to the flames.

The portico was certainly the best escape route available from the upper floor, though as the fire raged inside the building not everyone could make it to that side of the house. Some boys at the back of the house were required to jump from the upper windows onto the roof of an outhouse. At least one boy sustained broken legs from this initial jump before having to summon the courage for the second, excruciating jump to the ground.

Having made our own escape, we circled the building to see if we could do anything for those boys still trapped inside. At one end of the house, I noticed three boys standing on a narrow first floor balcony. They hadn't had time to grab sheets or blankets and as the fire raged inside they had no route to the ground other than a perilous jump which would almost certainly incur broken legs. To protect themselves from the fire, these boys had stood a mattress on its end in the window frame between them and it, but I could see that this would very shortly catch fire and that time was running out for them. I persuaded them to throw the mattress down to where I was standing and I hastily built up a plinth of snow on which to lay it. One by one the boys jumped down and the combined cushioning effect of mattress and snow ensured that each got up from his landing uninjured.

It was clear by now that the house was beyond saving. The fire had destroyed its telephone connection and there was no sign of the fire brigade. One boy, named Bland, made a heroic dash to Crediton to summon them. I think I remember seeing him set off on a bicycle but the newspapers would later report that he ran the mile and a half into town. He may have abandoned his bicycle, unable to keep the wheels turning through the thick snow. In the meantime, many of us who had escaped made for the estate's greenhouse in the American Garden, a safe distance from the inferno. A blizzard was blowing and the strong winds were fanning the flames which had, by now, engulfed the house. The greenhouse gave us relief from the cold as it was the only structure on the estate which was heated. We carried a boy there who had been very badly burned and was in great pain. We laid him on slabs in the greenhouse, trying to make him as comfortable as possible, but there was absolutely nothing else any of us could do for him until help arrived. Later that morning, the boy, Peter Charlesworth who was nine years old, was taken to the Royal Devon and Exeter Hospital: sadly, he died of his injuries two days later.

Eventually, probably having been alerted by Bland, the Crediton fire brigade arrived to great cheers and started to attack the blaze, drawing water from a large lake not far from the house. The firemen along with policemen, who arrived at the same time, rescued a further eighteen boys who were on top of the portico from which I had escaped earlier. The house was beyond saving and despite the arrival of fire crews from Exeter, Topsham and Tiverton all that could be done was to stop the blaze from spreading to nearby buildings. I will never forget the incredible noise when the roof fell in.

Shobrooke Park Mansion – the portico on the left side was my escape route. (Courtesy of Lost Heritage – England's Lost Country Houses www.lostheritage.co.uk)

After the fire had eventually been extinguished, three bodies were recovered from the ground floor. One was the school nurse, Emily Bell, a fifty-seven year old spinster; the others were boys whom I knew quite well. Charlie Gurdon, who had just turned eight, was the son of my godfather, Robin Gurdon who was killed in action near El Alamein in 1942 while serving with the Long Range Desert Group. His father's death had left Charlie heir to his family's title and had he lived he would have become the 3rd Baron Cranworth. The other boy, (Robert) Charles Sheffield, was nine and second in line to the Sheffield baronetcy. At the inquest following the fire, one lad testified that Nurse Bell had tried to lead some boys through a doorway: only Charlie Gurdon followed her, the rest were beaten back by the flames. Counsel for the mother of one of the boys maintained that all three probably died on the upper floor of the house and fell when the floor gave way. I believe this not to be the case and that those who lost their lives had all been trapped on the ground floor.

While the injured were taken to hospital, arrangements were swiftly made to accommodate those of us who had escaped unscathed. The two Crediton schools, the High School and the Queen Elizabeth Grammar, were quick to offer assistance and we were ferried there by a number of cars which made frequent journeys to and fro. I went to the latter which looked after us wonderfully well, feeding us and lending us clothes, while our parents were notified and travelled to collect us. My mother came for me and we took the train back to Salisbury, sharing a compartment with another boy from the school, named Livingstone, and his father. My mother had brought a flask of coffee with her which, by that time, had gone cold. She poured the coffee out of the carriage window only to see it blow back in all over the crisp uniform of Livingstone's father, a lieutenant-commander in the Navy. The incident provided a brief moment of amusement in an otherwise harrowing day.

The subsequent inquest into the fire was something of a

whitewash. The school's headmaster, Mr Ridgeway, told the court that he had not instituted regular fire drills within the house for fear of panicking the boys and because he thought it unwise to train them to take a prescribed route of escape. Until June of the previous year, he had employed a night watchman, but this man had left due to an eye problem and Ridgeway maintained he had been unable to find a suitable replacement. The cause of the fire was never conclusively established. Shobrooke had no mains electricity supply and was lit by gas mantles. Gas was often in short supply during the war and it had been off for some days prior to the fire. It is not difficult to imagine the fire being started by a carelessly placed candle. One other likely explanation emerged at the inquest. There had been a small fire in a storeroom a day or two earlier and it was suggested that a smouldering piece of matchboard from this first fire might have dropped between floorboards. The strong winds on the night of 23 January might have, it was maintained, whipped up the embers from this matchboard, causing the second, catastrophic fire. The Coroner ultimately recorded a verdict of 'Death by Misadventure' but attached no blame to the school, concluding, 'I very greatly sympathise with Mr Ridgeway and the boys' relations.' Of course, the war was in its final year and people had perhaps grown a little inured to bad news. Fire regulations and health and safety legislation didn't exist in those days but the inescapable truth is that the school was negligent in its care of us. Letters of support from a number of parents certainly weighed in Ridgeway's favour and he could also count on the endorsement of Queen Mary, whose sons, the Dukes of Gloucester and Kent had attended St Peter's Court and who wrote in support of the school.

After the fire, I spent some time at home and do not recall the events of that dramatic night having a profound effect on me, though Sarah thought I remained shaken and a little withdrawn for some time to follow. At this time, she was at Southover School, Lewes and was good friends with Jeryl Gurdon, the elder sister of Charlie, one of the fire's victims. The weekend after the fire, she noticed a story relating to it in a Sunday newspaper, copies of which were lying on a table in the hall waiting to be collected by staff. Sarah gathered the papers together and put them out of sight behind the back door so that Jeryl wouldn't see the story. I have always thought this an act of great compassion and kindness.

With Shobrooke gutted and awaiting demolition and with Broadstairs still unsafe, temporary arrangements were made to continue our education. Parents of boys stepped in to help and I was sent to Southover, the home of Jeremy Bellville who was a couple of years older than me, in Tolpuddle, Dorset. There were perhaps ten of us in total at Southover and two masters. Jeremy was great fun and completely unpredictable and we began a friendship that would last well beyond our school years. I saw the school year out at Southover and then, with the war over, the school reunited at Broadstairs. I remained at St Peter's Court until 1947 but was never really happy there.

During the time I was at Southover, I became concerned that I had not heard from my father for some time. After he left for France following D-Day, I received letters from him fairly regularly and then, suddenly, nothing. This would not have been long after we had received the terrible news of Michael's death in France and I feared that my father had also been killed and that my family were keeping this from me. The truth, when I learned it, was barely less difficult to accept. In 1944, before he headed off to Europe, my father had met and fallen in love with Mary Wyndham, a girl sixteen years his junior, the daughter of Brigadier Humphrey Wyndham, aide-de-camp to King George VI during the early years of the war. I was oblivious to all this, though Sarah has since told me that there were many hushed conversations among my mother, her sisters and my grandmother at Clarendon during this period. I don't recall who eventually broke the news to me or when. I think I may have been told while at Southover and that it was, perhaps, one of my teachers who broke the news, though it may have been my mother. It came as a great shock and upset me deeply. My father never came to Clarendon again and my parents divorced in 1945. Divorce was much rarer in those days and, like most children that age, it hadn't even occurred to me that my parents might one day separate.

After the war my father returned to Justerini & Brooks but not to 56 Rutland Gate which was my mother's house and which she sold. He and Mary married in Westminster in 1945 and settled in the country, my father commuting to London. They had two children, my half-brother, David in 1946 and half-sister, Charlotte in 1949. I was not introduced to Mary until I was in my first year at Eton in 1947. Her brother, Michael, who later became a great friend of mine, was in his last half, and my father and Mary came to the Fourth of June celebrations, Eton's best-known holiday held every year on the birthday of George III, the school's greatest patron. In the intervening period, I only recall my father coming to see me once. I was at Broadstairs, and he came to take me out one weekend. We went to Royal St George's golf course at nearby Sandwich, a regular venue for the Open Championship, where he was a member and I followed him round as he tested his game on one of country's most exacting links courses.

At about the time I was getting ready to go to Eton my mother moved to Kent, buying Stonehall, a red-bricked Queen Anne house in the village of Great Mongeham, two miles inland from Deal. I was never sure why she chose Kent, particularly as I was just about to leave for Eton. She certainly didn't stay there long, moving to Marlow in 1948 or 1949. I have few memories of the place but I do recall setting off from there in the middle of August 1948 to see the fifth and final Test of the Ashes Series. It was Don Bradman's last Test in England and, as it turned out, his last appearance for Australia. Needing just four runs to secure a Test batting average of one hundred, he was famously bowled for a duck by England leg spinner, Eric Hollies. I witnessed the most famous dismissal in the history of the game.

I went up to Eton in the spring of 1947 when I was still twelve having passed the Common Entrance Examination. I took the Upper Fourth form, one below the top, Remove, and this was quite unusual for a boy not yet thirteen and almost certainly better than I might have achieved had I stayed at Ludgrove. Despite its academic merits, I was quite pleased to see the back of St Peter's Court and to be reunited with many of the friends from whom I had been separated when I left Ludgrove. My cousin, Patrick Cobbold, who was the same age as me, also went to Eton at the same time. Even so, in those days, one's first day at Eton was quite daunting. I was simply dropped off, shown to my room and left to get on with it. There was certainly no friendly induction as there is today. Fortunately, I had older friends there who were able to show me the ropes. Jeremy Bellville and Richard (Dicken) Lumley, later Lord Scarborough, tracked me down and showed me around the place. This was very kind of them and it helped me to settle more quickly at Eton than would have otherwise been the case.

I thoroughly enjoyed my time at Eton. My housemaster, Jack Peterson, the man who persuaded my parents to send me to St Peter's Court, made a great impression on me and was adored by all those in his care. We were devastated when he left to become head of Shrewsbury School, a great honour because he was an Old Salopian. We gave his replacement, Donald Bousfield, something of a hard time. This was a little unfair; Peterson was so popular that anyone would have found it difficult to step into his shoes. Mr Bousfield held his house for seventeen years and eventually became just as popular as his predecessor.

I didn't do anything very distinguished at Eton, either in the classroom or on the sports field. I was not fond of Classics and dropped Greek and Latin as soon as I was able, preferring modern languages. I was neither a genius nor a dunce but was perhaps just above average in my class. Unlike my friends who had been to Ludgrove, I hadn't played much sport and consequently I didn't make any of the school teams. Nonetheless, I enjoyed playing cricket, the field game and was not bad at fives. I also had some success on the river as a cox with a bumping four. A bumping race is a game in which a number of boats set off down the river in single file, the aim of each crew being to bump or draw alongside the boat in front without falling victim to the boat behind. At Eton, one is either a 'dry bob' who plays cricket during the summer or a 'wet bob' who rows. Though I was a dry bob, I was quite small and very light and therefore an obvious choice as cox for these river games and I steered my crew to a number of wins.

I was not particularly well-behaved at Eton, getting involved in occasional low level mischief without ever gaining notoriety among the staff. Fortunately, I retained the happy knack from my earlier childhood for getting away with things and I seldom received sanction for my antics. Indeed I was in the 'Library' for my House, meaning that I was among the top six boys and acted as a prefect with some responsibility for maintaining discipline within the House. Without question, I will remember Eton most for its sense of camaraderie and for the dozens of wonderful friends I made there. Many of these friendships have lasted for more than sixty years, have seen me through some difficult times and have enriched my life enormously.

Sadly, I lost one of my great childhood friends during my first summer holiday from Eton. Giles Fox-Strangways, who was two days younger than me and who, if he were alive today, would be Lord Ilchester, often stayed with us at Clarendon during the holidays and I would sometimes stay with him at his house, Melbury, near Evershot in Dorset. On the last Saturday of August 1947, Giles, having just returned home from a few days with me at Clarendon, had been out shooting grey squirrels in woods on his family's estate. Later, he was seen cycling towards home, holding his airgun by the stock with the barrel pointing in the air. Shortly afterwards, he was found lying in the road with his gun beside him, dazed but conscious, by a GWR signalman, Joseph Vincent. The road was full of potholes and Vincent assumed that one of these had caused Giles to lose his grip on the gun which then slipped through the spokes of his front wheel which was badly damaged. Vincent tended to a wound to Giles' head and the pair talked about cricket and other things while they waited for help to arrive. Giles was eventually taken to Yeovil Hospital where he remained lucid. He told doctors that he remembered getting off his bicycle to load his gun so that he could take a shot at a rook and that the next thing he knew he went weak at the knees and fell. He had no recollection of the gun going off. On that Saturday and the following day it was assumed that the small puncture wound to his head had been caused by gravel as he fell to the ground. Only on Monday did an X-ray reveal that a pellet from his airgun had lodged in his brain. There was absolutely nothing doctors could do and Giles died the following day. At the inquest into his death, a policeman demonstrated that Giles' gun was poorly balanced and liable to go off accidentally. Chillingly, when he banged the gun on the courtroom floor, the spring was released.

Messing about in Clarendon's swimming pool with my friend Giles Fox-Strangways (left) who died in tragic circumstances. (Photograph: Rosemary Crawley)

I spent five years at Eton. I left, aged seventeen, deciding not to stay on for the last half which would have taken me into sixth form. In the aftermath of war, National Service had been made compulsory and the question for boys my age was whether to join the army straight from school or to go to university first. I had gained all the necessary qualifications for university and a debate ensued as to whether I should follow my father to Cambridge or go, instead, to Oxford where all of my mother's family had studied. I settled the matter and decided to go to neither.

2. Into the Army

Before I began my National Service, I took something of a working holiday. Nowadays, this might be termed a 'gap' for I travelled through France, alternately working and relaxing. After I had left Eton, it was thought that I might eventually follow my father into the wine trade and it was he who made the arrangements for me to visit some of France's best wine houses in order to gain an understanding of viticulture and oenology and to meet people with influence in the industry. I left England in the late spring of 1952 and over the course of the following three months I spent time at four of France's most renowned wine houses where I was made very welcome indeed.

The first was in the Médoc village of Pauillac, thirty miles north-west of Bordeaux on the western bank of the Gironde – Château Mouton Rothschild, renowned producer of some of the world's finest clarets. I spent two weeks there in considerable comfort and was treated very kindly as a guest, not being asked to lift a finger. While I was there, Baron Philippe de Rothschild, whose house it was, came down for the weekend with a crowd of his very sophisticated friends. The Baron very kindly invited me to play tennis and bridge with his friends and he asked me to join them for grand dinner parties even though I was, at eighteen, much the youngest of his houseguests. He was a man of great energy, a racing driver, poet and patron of the arts and he made a great impression on me. During my stay, I spent a lot of time with his estate manager who took me under his wing and taught me a lot about the wine trade. Together, we travelled around visiting other châteaux and, in the short time I was there, I became familiar with other parts of the Bordeaux region. Later, towards the end of my tour of France, the Baron would invite me to a grand ball in Paris arranged in honour of his daughter, Philippine, though, to my regret, I was unable to attend. Sadly, Philippine died in August 2014.

From Mouton I went the short distance to the Quai des Chartrons in the heart of Bordeaux to Maison Calvet where I was put to work. I do not recall the precise nature of my duties there, but I was well looked after. Next I went to Hennessy's at Cognac as a guest, again staying in some comfort and not being required to work for my keep. All the while I was not only learning much about the production of and trade in wines and spirits but my French was also improving immeasurably. Later, when I was in Paris, it was remarked that I spoke French, not like an Englishman, but with a Bordelais accent. Though Bordelais is not the prettiest of French accents, I was flattered by the observation. My last visit and the place I stayed longest was at Ruinart, the oldest Champagne house, established in 1729 by Nicolas Ruinart in Rheims. There, I worked very hard in the cellars for about a month, carrying bottles from one place to another and sticking labels on. Again, my hosts were extraordinarily hospitable and when not working I was invited to lunch and dinner with the great and the good of the Champagne region, meeting, among others, Charles Heidsieck and Paul Krug.

Though I was not destined to work in the drinks industry, my time in France was immensely interesting and instructive. At that time of my life, having never smoked or drunk alcohol, my palate was perfectly clean and while in France I became adept at

Into the Army

distinguishing different wines through blind tasting. Sadly, I no longer retain this talent though I do remain discerning in my tastes.

I returned from France at about the end of July 1952 and joined the army a month or so later. I had already had a taste of military affairs having joined the Corps at Eton. Though this is now voluntary, during my time, it was more or less compulsory. In my final half, I was among those selected from the Eton Corps to form a guard of honour immediately outside the gates of St George's Chapel, Windsor as the funeral procession for King George VI set off. Of course there was already a tradition of military service from both sides of my family, particularly in their recent histories. Few English families could have given more of their sons in the service of their country than the Cobbolds. No fewer than thirty-five Cobbold men were killed during the course of the First World War, a further twelve in the Second and one woman, Barbara Elizabeth Cobbold, who died in London during the Blitz. Barbara was not the only civilian caught in the wrong place at the wrong time: Peter Charles Victor Cobbold, a manager with the Borneo Company Limited, was summarily executed in 1942 by Japanese marines. Peter, who worked at Sibu in Sarawak had fled the Japanese invasion of Borneo and headed for the jungle of the island's mountainous interior, along with other westerners, mostly British and Dutch. After six months spent at an abandoned Dutch military base at Long Nawang, the party's location was betrayed by natives and all seventy or so of the refugees, including some women and children were brutally massacred. The atrocity is considered one of the worst perpetrated by the Japanese during World War II: no one was ever held to account for it.

All but four of the '48', as they are known within my family, were killed while on active service. Many were of low rank and many fell with their friends in the mud of Flanders and the Somme. Perhaps the best known was my godfather Lieutenant-Colonel John Murray 'Ivan' Cobbold, head of the family brewing business and chairman of Ipswich Town Football Club. On Sunday 18 June 1944, Ivan, who had previously been wounded in the First World War, was attending a church service at the Guards' Chapel in Birdcage Walk where, twenty-five years earlier, he had married his wife, Lady Blanche Cavendish, daughter of the 9th Duke of Devonshire. The chapel was packed and shortly after 11 a.m. some in the congregation heard a faint buzzing in the distance.

The Guards' Chapel Bombing which claimed the life of my godfather, John Murray Cobbold.
(Courtesy of the Reverend Kevin Bell, Chaplain to the Household Division)

The buzz became louder and louder until it reached a roar overhead, drowning out the hymn singing. Then, the engine of the V1 rocket cut out and it fell directly onto the roof of the chapel,

Into the Army 53

detonating on impact. The entire roof fell onto the worshippers below. Ivan was one of 121 military personnel and civilians who lost their lives; a further 141 were injured, many seriously.

In November 2007, I travelled to London with my son, Robert, where we were joined by seven other Cobbolds, spanning three generations. On Remembrance Sunday, we marched together to the Cenotaph where we laid a wreath of poppies arranged around the family crest which bears the family motto, 'Rebus Angustis Fortis' – 'Strength in Adversity.' Attached to the wreath was a remembrance card which simply read '48 Cobbolds'. Tucked behind the card was a list of their names. The ceremony was deeply moving. The '48' do not, of course include those from my family and extended family who also lost their lives serving King and Country and were not Cobbolds, such as my beloved uncle, Michael Christie-Miller, my great uncle, Seymour Vandeleur, two of my godfathers and countless others.

Nine Cobbolds at the Cenotaph. L-R: David, Humphrey, Esther, Tim, Me, Jack, Robert (my son), Jeremy, Anthony.
(Photograph: The Cobbold Family History Trust)

Like my father, my uncle Michael and my great uncle, Edward Christie-Miller, I went into the Coldstream Guards. I went first to Caterham, in Surrey, for my basic training where I arrived in some style. I was friends with Tom Craig, the stepson of Dick Fairey, son of the founder of Fairey Aviation. Dick Fairey flew us into Croydon Airport, from where we were driven the short distance to Caterham. The comfort of our journey was in stark contrast to the regime and living conditions which awaited us. I shared a spartanly furnished dormitory in a Nissen hut with about thirty to forty other officer cadets reporting to an officer of the Coldstream, Captain Eddie Digby, whose task it was to knock us into shape. My cousin, Patrick Cobbold, who was exactly the same age as me was among my roommates. We had been in the same year at Eton (though not in the same House) and had become firm friends. Patrick was the youngest son of Ivan Cobbold, victim of the Guards' Chapel bombing. The trained soldier assigned to us always had difficulty in telling us apart and frequently got us mixed up. In his frustration, he resorted to calling us 'Nobbold fucking N' and 'Nobbold fucking P.'

We were certainly kept on our toes at Caterham and my main recollections of the place are of a gruelling cycle of polishing, pressing, kit inspections, drill and punishing runs, though I did find time to play the odd practical joke. Cleaning the windows of our Nissen hut was one of the regular chores we had to undertake. To liven things up a bit, I happened to mention to one of my peers that a better clean could be achieved by lighting the cleaning fluid, Windolene, or some such product. He blindly followed my advice, poured the fluid onto the pane and quickly struck a match before it ran off the glass: the ensuing bang was enough to cause him to fall from his perch on the window sill. Fortunately for him the sill was only three feet from the ground.

Of course, the object of this stage of our training was to transform boys into men, to make us fitter, more disciplined and to ready us for the next stage of our military education. In this it succeeded. Those of us who completed our basic training to the required standard went on to Eaton Hall, a large estate in Cheshire owned by the Duke of Westminster. In 1943, after the Britannia Royal Naval College at Dartmouth had been damaged by bombs, the Duke had made Eaton Hall, at the time vacant, available as a replacement. Regular naval officers were trained there until 1946. Thereafter, until 1958 when National Service was phased out, it served as a training college for conscripted officer cadets. Some fifteen thousand young men passed through its gates during that time, many destined for service in the world's hotspots such as Cyprus, Egypt, Korea, Malaya and Kenya. Most, like me, came from infantry divisions, though cadets from other Corps, including the Engineers and the Royal Marines, also passed through its gates. During our training, we wore our own regiment's uniform with white gorget tabs on the collar to identify us as cadets.

Officer training at Eaton Hall lasted for about sixteen weeks, divided into two phases. The first, or Primary Phase, gave training in 'basic military subjects' and assessed one's suitability to proceed to more specialised training leading to a commission. Once through the first phase, the aim of the Advanced Phase was to 'turn out an Infantry 2nd Lieutenant sufficiently grounded in all aspects of platoon and section training, company administration and general military knowledge so that, after further practical experience in a field unit, he can exercise effective command as a platoon officer.' Our training was conducted both in the classroom and in the field and I remember taking part in exercises at Trawsfynydd in North Wales where we were put through our paces, marching cross country, and often firing live rounds.

Patrick and I went to Eaton Hall together and I remember my time there being much more comfortable than the three or so months I had spent at Caterham. I completed the course successfully and remember having some fun in the process. On one occasion, I persuaded five of my friends to help me carry my car, a 1930s Wolseley Hornet which I had bought in London for £75, up the main steps of the house. Then, I got behind the wheel, started the engine and drove through the front door and into the main hall of the house. For some minutes I screeched in circles around the hall and careered down corridors and through at least one dormitory. This was not particularly easy as the Hornet had a very bad lock which made cornering and three-point turns quite difficult. Eventually, I made my exit and drove down the steps up which my friends and I had carried the car – bump, bump, bump. Remarkably, my indoor rally seemed not to have been witnessed by anyone in authority and I was never hauled over the coals for it or any of my other antics during my time at Eaton Hall. Among other incidents, I recall a particularly fierce water fight which raged in the hall and on the stairs for some time and which involved the use of at least one fire extinguisher: fortunately, the Duke had had the prescience to remove most of his furniture and valuable pieces before handing Eaton Hall over to the forces but I do remember that one valuable painting, a Reubens, too large to be removed from the main hall, was splashed during this skirmish.

Despite being at the heart of such japes, I was considered sufficiently responsible to take on additional duties and was selected as one of only two or three junior under officers in my group. My great hope while training at Eaton Hall was to go to Korea. I knew Colonel Arthur Fortescue, who was to command the Coldstream battalion there, personally and I asked him if he would consider taking me with him. He agreed but, as the war fizzled out into stalemate in the first half of 1953, I was never called upon to go. It would not be the last time that my desire to see action with the army would come to nought.

My training complete, I must have spent a short time during the summer of 1953 at home with my mother in Marlow, before I received my posting with the 3rd Coldstream in Egypt. During the Second World War, Egypt had been an important base for British operations in North Africa and in the Mediterranean. Large numbers of troops remained there after the war but were withdrawn to the areas around the Suez Canal, which continued to be controlled by Britain and France. In 1952 a nationalist revolution led by General Neguib overthrew the decrepit, pro-British ruler, King Farouk and, in early 1953, Neguib demanded that all British troops leave Egyptian territory. The British Government, under Churchill, refused to evacuate the Canal Zone and a tense stand-off ensued. Egyptian raids against British positions on the canal became commonplace and British civilians and their families living in the country were harassed. As tensions mounted, war between Britain and Egypt seemed a distinct possibility. This was the state of affairs in Egypt when I was flown in to command my platoon at the height of summer in 1953.

We flew from Stansted and the journey was far from comfortable. The aeroplane was an old bomber, retired from service, which had been used for aerial filming the previous day. The filming had required windows to be removed so that pictures could be captured unobstructed and, to our misfortune, some of these had not been replaced properly. Conditions on board were draughty to say the least and we were glad to be in full battle dress. We were able to warm up a bit as the plane landed at Malta to take on fuel but most of the journey was spent shivering with teeth chattering. In contrast, conditions when we landed in Egypt at an army base near Fayid were unbearably hot and we couldn't wait to swap our heavy battle dress for desert fatigues. Fayid, which lies towards the southern end of the Suez Canal where it bulges into the Great Bitter Lake, was to be my base for the next four or so months.

When I arrived, nineteen years old and an ensign (second lieutenant), I didn't know any of the officers in my battalion. We lived in tents and I soon got to know them all quite well and enjoyed their company. I commanded a platoon of twenty-five to thirty men with whom I also got on well. We were on a high state of alert, ready to be called to march on Cairo at two hours' notice should the need arise; our bags were always packed, ready to move and one would even take one's rifle or pistol to the lavatory. In the event of war, we would make for Cairo as quickly as possible in convoy. Rather than fight our way up the banks of the canal it was considered better to drive quickly and run the gauntlet of the Egyptian forces and Fedayeen fighters. In the event that we were mobilised, I was allocated a seat in the lead vehicle of this convoy that would be many miles long, conveying tens of thousands of men. This was a somewhat dubious privilege as I would certainly have been at the most vulnerable end of the column. Either my superiors considered me one of their more capable young officers or one of the most expendable. Thankfully, during my tour, neither the sights of the Egyptian forces nor the Fedayeen were ever trained on me.

Once we had got used to being in an almost constant state of alert, camp life could become a little monotonous and dull, though the camaraderie of one's men and fellow officers provided many moments of light relief. I made good use of any leave afforded to me. Once I travelled with some other officers across the Sinai Desert to Aqaba and from there to the ancient city of Petra. This was long before that breathtakingly beautiful ancient city became one of the world's most popular tourist destinations. Now visitors have to jostle for the best views of the city with some of the hundreds of thousands of travellers who go there each year: we had the place to ourselves and it was absolutely stunning. We climbed to the top of the hill beyond Petra and looked down on the valley below – purported to be the land of milk and honey into which Moses led the Israelites as described in the Book of Exodus. On another occasion, I took a couple of days off and travelled north to Port Said, at the mouth of the canal, to see my cousin, Patrick, who was there with the Scots Guards. One evening, we were sitting in a slit trench together just twenty yards from the canal which, being built up, was above our position so that we couldn't see the water. All of a sudden an enormous passenger liner glided serenely past our position, so close to us that I could have thrown an orange on board. From where we were sitting we couldn't see any of the ship's hull, just the brightly illuminated decks which towered above us. We could hear music and see people dancing as parties went on inside, the passengers completely unaware of our presence so close. We even saw a couple engaged in a tryst behind one of the lifeboats. Patrick and I were transfixed as the ship inched past us; it was one of the most spellbinding sights either of us had ever seen.

Such interludes provided much needed relief from the tedium of day to day life at Fayid. I never received the call to mount the three-tonner which would lead the British assault on Cairo and my short tour came to an end in late 1953 without major incident. My journey to Egypt had been an uncomfortable one and my journey home, by ship rather than aeroplane, was no pleasure cruise either. The HMTS (Her Majesty's Troopship) *Lancashire,* with one very high funnel, was a veteran of both world wars and had been the commodore ship for the landings on Juno beach on D-Day. Nearly ten years on, she was coming to the end of her working life: I confess there were times when I thought that my life might come to an end with her. She had a pronounced list to the port side and I firmly believe that it was only the strong westerly winds battering the Bay of Biscay as we headed home which kept her upright. We were at sea for Christmas and during the course of the festivities plenty of those on board the *Lancashire* developed a pronounced list too. Tradition has it that the officers serve the men their Christmas lunch and this we did. We all had a merry time. We ate well and had plenty to drink, though in rough seas this led to inevitable consequences: as the boat heaved in the rough seas of the Bay of Biscay, so did most of her passengers.

Into the Army

HMTS *Lancashire*. (Courtesy of the Lindy Lovegrove Collection)

The *Lancashire* remained upright and made it to Liverpool between Christmas and New Year. I was given the honour of carrying the colour off the boat to be greeted by our colonel, George Burns. We boarded a train for London and Wellington Barracks where I was to see out the remainder of my National Service. Army life in London was quite different to that I had experienced in Egypt. We trained for various guards and I did them all; Buckingham Palace, St James' Palace, the Tower of London, Trooping the Colour, the Bank Picket and lining the Mall when important foreign dignitaries were visiting. The Bank Picket was perhaps the most fun, requiring one officer to lead thirty men through London's busy streets. We would march through Admiralty Arch, down Whitehall, along the Embankment and up to Threadneedle Street, a distance of between two and three miles; we didn't pause for the traffic, hoping that it would give way to us. We would arrive just as the Bank was closing for the evening and getting through the door could be quite tricky against a distracting tide of young typists and office girls leaving for home. Once in, all was very civilised. As officer in charge of the picket, I was very well looked after. I was allowed to invite one male guest to dine with me in a private room. A sumptuous meal was provided and accompanied by claret and port. The guest was assumed to be *bona fide* by the Bank and no checks were made against him, though he had to leave the premises by about 11 o'clock. All that was really required of me was to make a tour of the building at around midnight and check with my men that everything was in order. In the morning we would then march back to the barracks. Officers did the Bank Picket on a rota; I did it on a number of occasions and always looked forward to it. Duty at the Tower of London was rather more tedious, though at least we didn't have to march there. Arriving in a three-tonner, we would be there all day and time dragged as there was very little to do. Once, to ease the boredom, I decided to conduct a scientific experiment with one of the Tower's famous feathered residents, its ravens. I soaked a piece of bread in some whisky, fed it to a raven, and stood back to observe the effects. Before long the unfortunate bird began staggering about on one of the perimeter walls, pissed, until it lost its balance altogether and simply fell off.

I was glad to have had done all the guards duties once, though think I may have become bored if asked to do them for two summers in a row. Perhaps the most memorable moment came when I was asked to carry the Queen's Colour at the Royal Tournament at Earls Court in 1954. The Colour had not come out since before the war and it was so lavishly embroidered that it was very heavy to carry. To ensure I got things right on the night and to avoid risking damage to the Colour, I practised at Wellington Barracks with a large blanket with lead sown into it to simulate its weight. The first time I picked this up, a gust of wind caught the blanket and blew me some twenty yards to the right. Fortunately, there was no wind inside Earls Court to throw me off balance when I came to carry the Colour in front of Her Majesty and all went well.

Of course, ceremonial duties took up only so much of our time in London and we were engaged in ordinary soldiering duties as well. Off duty, there was great fun to be had, particularly during the London season of balls and parties. My grandmother very generously provided me with an allowance of £300 per year from the time I left Eton until I left the army in the early autumn of 1954. This enabled me to take a flat just off Pont Street near Sloane Square, which I shared with my old childhood friend, Christopher Thynne, who was with the Life Guards. The flat gave us greater freedom to enjoy London's nightlife when we were off duty. Whether I was staying in barracks or at the flat, the bright lights of the West End were hard to resist. On one occasion, when I was on duty as picket officer, I slipped out to a night club; when I returned to barracks several hours later, I remembered, to my horror, that I had left my picket cane in the club and had to dash back to retrieve it.

I had, by this time, replaced my Wolseley Hornet with a Ford Popular, a car which was ubiquitous on England's roads during the 1950s and 1960s and, at £400, just about the cheapest car one could buy new. I decided that a race would be a good idea and persuaded three other young officers, who also owned Populars, to take part; Peter Wilmot-Sitwell was one, the others were Christopher Willoughby and Nicholas 'Sam' Baring. Wellington Barracks was to be our starting point and the winner would be the first to reach my mother's house at Marlow. There were no other rules and we were each free to take whichever route we liked. As we sat in our cars, revving and waiting for the off, an immediate problem became apparent; the gateway at the barracks was only just wide enough for two cars to get through. Fortunately, I got away quickly, as did Peter and we made it out onto the street first. Baring was forced to give way, while Willoughby, in attempting to squeeze through a gap which simply wasn't there ploughed into the sentry box, his race over almost as soon as it had begun. Though I was quickest away, it was clear that Peter was going to be my closest rival. Near Shepherd's Bush I took an ingenious short cut in order to press home my early advantage. I drove onto the forecourt of a filling station, its pump attendants assuming I was stopping for petrol: I didn't stop at all and drove through to the back of the garage where the mechanics thought I was coming in for a service. I drove straight through the premises, front to back, without stopping, cutting off a whole corner and giving myself an unassailable lead. I reached Marlow well ahead of Peter with Sam Baring, tailed off, a further quarter of an hour behind. Waiting for us at the finishing line were my twin sisters, Clare and Anne, then almost sixteen. It was the first time they had met Peter, a dashing nineteen-year-old, who had been in the year below me at Eton. Over the following few years, romance blossomed between Clare and Peter and they married in 1960. I may have won the race but

Into the Army

With my future brother-in-law, Peter Wilmot-Sitwell after our race in Ford Populars to my mother's house in Marlow.

Peter has always maintained, quite rightly, that he won the prize.

When my two years were up, in the late summer of 1954, Colonel George Burns very kindly asked me to stay on as a regular. By this time, I had decided that university wasn't for me. The army had made a man of me and, having commanded thirty men in the desert under near battle conditions, I was some way ahead of my contemporaries who had chosen to go to university first. Though I had enjoyed my National Service immensely and was flattered by Colonel Burns' offer, I realised that I needed to start making my way in the world and earning some money. My first thought was to go into the City and I sought the advice of an old family friend, Arthur James. After leaving the Grenadier Guards, Arthur had become a stockbroker with Sebag where he had done quite well. I asked him whether he would recommend the profession. He advised me that I should give it a go and he very kindly offered to keep his ear to the ground and to let me know should any suitable opportunities arise. Before long and, having been tipped off by Arthur, I was offered a position with the stockbroking firm, Williams de Broë.

The offices of Williams de Broë were in Pinners Hall, Austin Friars in the City. Formed in 1869, the company was rich in tradition and this was reflected in its oak-panelled offices and by its partners, who on the whole, were all knocking on a bit. I joined the company at the most junior level though it was understood that I would be groomed to become a partner one day. With this in mind, the company made arrangements for me to learn every aspect of the City and of stockbroking by giving me experience with other companies. First, I went to a chartered accountant in London for a few months to learn something about figures and then I was sent to a country broker in Newcastle to learn about the Stock Exchange. The company, Boys-Stones, Simpson and Spencer, looked after me very well and, while in Newcastle, I stayed in great comfort at the Northern Counties Club on Eldon Square. The partners of the company asked me to shoot with them and to stay with them at weekends, sometimes offering me a horse so that I could hunt with them. Other landowners in the area also invited me to shoot and afforded me the same courtesy. I spent several enjoyable months up there and when I returned to London some months later, I had a decent grasp of the profession I had chosen to take up.

Whilst in Newcastle I also learned to fly. I started taking lessons at Newcastle Airport for three reasons. Firstly, I had always wanted to fly; secondly I got fed up of taking lunch on my own and learning taking lessons seemed a much better use of my lunch hour; thirdly, there was a very attractive air hostess at the airport, called Prim, whom I was keen to get to know better. I think I must have got my love of flying from my mother, though unlike her, I faced no opposition from my parents. The airport at that time was close to the centre of Newcastle and I spent as much time in the air as I could, eventually I got my Private Pilot's Licence: I also got the girl.

The Auster, the plane in which I learned to fly, was not particularly fast and I remember one particularly amusing incident which occurred while I was flying up to Scotland to visit a female friend. I hadn't bothered to take any maps with me, instead following the course of the northbound A1, flying at perhaps seventy miles per hour. All of a sudden a car on the road below overtook (or perhaps more precisely, undertook) me. I was not used to being overtaken on the road let alone when I was flying: when I first travelled up to Newcastle from Maidenhead in my Ford Popular I had not been passed once. Now, as I looked down on the speeding driver who had shown the audacity to outpace me, I was determined to exact my revenge. Seeing that he would have to slow down as he approached a roundabout, I set the Auster into a dive and gave him the fright of his life. My wheels must have been just twenty feet above his windscreen as I pulled the nose up and roared off into the distance. Wisely, or perhaps because he was in a state of shock, the driver decided to withdraw from our little race.

Back in London and with a much better knowledge of stockbroking than I had had before I went to Newcastle, my career with Williams de Broë began to take off. I started off as a Blue Button, or runner, the lowest form of life at the Stock

Exchange. Blue Buttons were not members of the Stock Exchange but were allowed in. We worked in what was known as 'a box', a small dealing room with space for about six or eight people who would be running in and out, telephoning and making trades on behalf of the partners who were upstairs in the offices. I enjoyed the cut and thrust of trading and started to do quite well. After Newcastle, I had returned to my flat off Pont Street which I continued to share with Christopher Thynne. We enjoyed what London had to offer and had great fun attending parties and frequenting nightclubs. We enjoyed some luck with the ladies and, at the flat, we developed a signalling system for one to indicate to the other the measure of this success. If one should walk through the front door to see a flowerpot turned upside down in the hallway, he knew the other was not to be disturbed.

The tenant in the flat below us was a strikingly beautiful aspiring actress called Lola. Lola had a penchant for exotic pets and was sometimes to be seen walking around the West End with a pet rat in a cage instead of a handbag. Christopher and I had very little to do with her except for one bizarre incident which occurred while I was at work. Christopher was sitting in the flat passing the time of day when he heard a knock on the front door. He opened the door to find Lola on the doorstep wearing only a dressing gown, her hair dripping wet having just emerged from the shower. Christopher, who always had an eye for a pretty girl, was struck dumb by this vision of beauty in front of him; even more so when Lola fixed his gaze and uttered six words that I don't think he'll ever forget, 'Have you seen my bush....baby?' One can only imagine the disappointment Christopher felt when Lola delivered the final word after a tantalising pause. I don't

Into the Army 69

think Lola's acting career ever really took off though she did land a part in an Italian film in the mid-sixties. At some point during this time, Christopher and I moved flats. In between moving out of our old flat and moving into the new one, we spent a week at the Cavendish Hotel in Jermyn Street. At that time, the Cavendish was run by Edith Jeffrey, a friend of its well-known owner Rosa Lewis who had died a few years earlier. Edith knew our parents well and put us up at the Cavendish for just £5 a night.

I kept up with my flying back in London and would often take to the skies from White Waltham airfield, which was not far from my mother's house at Marlow. It was from there that I took off in a Tiger Moth on the morning of Saturday 5 May, 1956: it was my 22nd birthday and, as things turned out, very nearly my last. My flight path that morning took me south to the village of Dummer in Hampshire where my father lived. There was nowhere to land in the village but I had come prepared and as my father came out into his garden to wave at me, I dive bombed and pelted him with eggs and loo rolls. My bombing mission complete, I turned north and made back for White Waltham and home. I didn't make it. Not far from Theale, just west of Reading, my engine cut out without warning. Losing height, I just managed to clear a belt of trees which bordered a field in which were held in a number of sheep pens. The engine briefly spluttered into life again but my relief was short-lived. Just as I thought I might be able to extend the plane's glide and land it safely, I lost power for a second and final time. The plane went into a spin and plummeted into the ground not far from the sheep. As I fell out of the sky, I was absolutely convinced I would be killed on impact and remember wondering how different the next life would be from the one which was about to end and how the transition between the two would take place. Despite the seemingly hopeless situation I was in, I was not at all afraid.

I never lost consciousness. The Tiger Moth has two seats and, if one is flying alone, one always takes the rear seat. Had I been sitting forward I would have been killed instantly as the front of the plane absorbed most of the impact telescoping the other cockpit. My face smashed into the dashboard with some force but I was otherwise uninjured and managed to get out onto one of the wings and jump clear of the wreck. Not long afterwards, a couple who had seen the plane fall out of the sky came running over to help, but came to an abrupt halt about fifty yards from me when they saw the extent of the injuries to my face which was covered in blood. They shouted that they would fetch the emergency services, turned around and ran off in the direction from which they had come. The police were the first on the scene and I was still with the plane. On seeing me as they ran across the field they shouted, 'Stand back! It's going to go up any minute!' 'I shouldn't think so', I replied, 'It's been cold on the ground for half an hour.' I later learned that the field I had crashed into belonged to William Benyon, a Berkshire landowner who later became a Member of Parliament: he never thanked me for avoiding his sheep.

I was taken to Reading Battle Hospital, where the care I received was not the best. Frustrated, I got out of bed and made for the exit and found a public telephone on the street from where I called home. My mother was away and she had given the house over to me for the weekend so I had half a dozen or so friends to stay. X-rays had been taken and the hospital told me that nothing was broken and that I could leave. My friends collected me and took me home. I was in considerable discomfort, unable to eat and only able to drink through a straw. When my mother returned home the following day, Sunday, she was quite shocked at my appearance and took a very poor view of the treatment I had received at Reading. First thing on Monday morning, she took me to Windsor Hospital where the full extent of my injuries was revealed: besides the more obvious damage to my teeth, my cheek bone was smashed in sixteen places and my eye-socket and jaw bone broken. The doctors there were aghast that I had been discharged from hospital on Saturday.

It was clear that I would need some reconstructive surgery and my mother got straight on to my uncle Sammy, who was chairman of the Wiltshire Hospitals. To my great fortune, Sammy was able to call upon the services of the world's leading plastic surgeon who, as luck would have it, specialised in facial reconstruction. John Barron, a New Zealander, had established the Wessex Regional Plastic and Maxillo-Facial unit at Odstock Hospital in Salisbury in 1949. The unit was the best in the world and attracted students from many countries. In 1953 Barron became president of the British Association of Plastic Surgeons, BAPS, and he truly was one of the great pioneers of cosmetic surgery. My mother rushed me from Windsor to Salisbury where Mr Barron dropped everything on my behalf, examined me briefly and concluded that he needed to operate immediately. I was on the operating table for several hours, during which time Mr Barron drilled through, wired up and reset my features. He did a very good job and I owe him a great debt of gratitude.

While I was recovering, tensions in Egypt were deepening. On 26 July 1956, General Nasser announced his decision to nationalise the Suez Canal which, hitherto, had been controlled by Britain and France. Nationalisation of the canal posed a great threat to British commercial and military interests in the region and a cross-party consensus quickly emerged that military action was required. Troops were mobilised on 2 August. Though I hadn't seen action during my National Service, I thought the experience I had gained in Egypt would be of use to the army and I determined to re-join. During my tour of the country I had been frustrated that we had been unable to fire back at an enemy which was firing at British troops at will and the latest developments conjured images in my mind of rape and loot in Alexandria. In short, I was desperate to return and to see some action. However, one thing stood in my way. As the crisis unfolded, the prime minister, Anthony Eden, stood up in the House of Commons and asserted that Britain's response would be handled by the regular army and that there was no need to call on the reserve. Despite this, I advanced on regimental headquarters in Birdcage Walk, approached the regimental adjutant and informed him that I wanted to come back. 'We can't take you back', was the adjutant's immediate response and he went on to cite Eden's statement to the House. 'Aren't I more use to you than someone who hasn't left Pirbright?' came my response. He was unable to deny that this was the case so I quickly followed up with the question, 'Does the army ever make mistakes?' 'Yes', he replied. I hammered home my advantage, 'Well let them make one now!' I said. Two days later, I received a telegram calling me back.

I was given a platoon to command straight away. My

platoon sergeant, named Badham, was a first class soldier as were all those who served under us. Most, like me, were reservists who had come back, though we were soon able to out-shoot and out-march the regular army. I would dearly have loved to have fought with these men but our chance never came. We got as far as Shorncliffe in Kent, where we painted our trucks sand-coloured, fully expecting to be sent to Egypt. The crisis came to a head in early November when British, French and Israeli troops invaded Egypt, intent on seizing control of the canal. On 7 November, the UN Assembly voted 65 to 1 that the invading powers should quit Egyptian territory and a humiliating climb-down ensued. Many historians consider the crisis to be the point which confirmed the loss of Britain's status as a great world power.

While we were waiting for the call, my platoon continued to train. During one training exercise, I, and some of my men, managed to get into the camp of the 'enemy' where we liberated a number of thunder flashes. These are baton-shaped fireworks designed to simulate a grenade going off without causing harm. To deploy a thunder flash, the top is removed and a striker within it is used to light a short fuse. It is then thrown towards the enemy and gives off a very loud bang, emitting a plume of smoke. In effect, a thunder flash is to a grenade what a blank is to a bullet. At the time, I wasn't sure what I would do with my stash, but I was sure they would come in handy one day.

Not long afterwards, I was waiting to use a telephone box at Pirbright Camp in Surrey. The box was occupied and I was becoming anxious as I was shortly due on parade and the call was of some importance. I paced around impatiently as the soldier inside the box, Peter Drinkwater, seemed either oblivious to my presence or unwilling to curtail his call so that I could make mine. Eventually, I decided to take matters into my own hands. I took out a thunder flash, lit the fuse, opened the door to the box and lobbed it in, allowing Drinkwater to make a hasty escape. If my aim was to free up the box, my plan worked. Unfortunately for me, the force of the explosion ripped the telephone clean off the wall and I never did get to make my call.

Another opportunity to have some fun with a thunder flash presented itself that winter when we were at Pickering Camp in North Yorkshire on live firing exercises. One evening I was in the officer's mess, a Nissen hut, trying to relax after a hard day in the field. There was only one other officer in the mess who was warming his feet on the stove in the middle of the room. To my intense annoyance this man was running through his entire repertoire of bugle calls, making an irritating 'peep, peep, peeping' noise. This had been going on for about half an hour and was beginning to drive me mad. I decided enough was enough and thought of a plan that was sure to shut him up. I crept outside without him noticing and began to climb stealthily up the curved roof of the hut. It was very cold, but this worked to my advantage as the roof was covered in six inches of snow which muffled the sound of my progress, making it impossible for the 'peeper' to hear me. Having reached the top of the roof, I steadied myself, whipped out a thunder flash, lit it and dropped it down the chimney. It went off spectacularly when it reached the fire below wrecking the stove on which the unfortunate man was still resting his feet. The explosion must have nearly blown his balls off.

In addition to the fine companionship of my battalion, there was another who went everywhere with me during my second stint in the army and on whose loyalty I could always count: my faithful whippet, Dan. Of course, pets weren't usually allowed in the army and I'm not quite sure how I managed to get round the rules; I think I just turned up at Shorncliffe with him and no objection was raised. I was certainly the only one of thirty or so officers there to have a dog. Very quickly, Dan became my battalion's unofficial mascot and all the men loved him. He would come with us on marches and exercises, night and day. On one such occasion I returned to camp to find the men cooking a rabbit using a bayonet over an open fire; the rabbit had been caught and delivered by Dan. Later, when we were making our way back to Kent from Pickering, Dan travelled with my platoon battalion in a three-tonner as the open jeep which I drove would have been too cold for him. We were supposed to drive in convoy but I suggested that we each make our own way and meet up in a pub just outside the camp at Shorncliffe. Dan and the others beat me back and settled down to eat. When I eventually arrived, Dan, who was curled up on one of the guardsman's laps, noticed me and took the shortest possible route to greet me. He leaped straight across the table, sending cutlery, glasses and plates of ham, eggs and bacon off in every direction. Oblivious to the carnage he had left in his wake, he jumped into my arms.

With Suez resolved and not much fancying the prospect of clicking my heels in the army until another conflict arose, I decided to leave and return to the City. Colonel George Burns, now commander of the 4th Guards Brigade (and now a brigadier), again asked me to stay on, but my mind was made up that I ought to return to Williams de Broë and carve out a career for myself in the City. I returned to my flat in London. Christopher Thynne was no longer staying there having gone off to America, but I sometimes had another old school friend as company, Jeremy Bellville. Jeremy was great fun and very predictable; he lived abroad quite a lot but would occasionally turn up in London out of the blue. In the time since we had been at school, he had joined the Fleet Air Arm and had seen action in Korea. He was a daring flyer, and his antics got him into all sorts of trouble on one occasion. Though he didn't have a civil licence, he once hired a plane near his home on the south coast and flew across to the Isle of Wight where his family had a house. Over the Solent he saw a boat engaged in pulling up the sea defences which had been placed during the war. He set his plane into a dive and passed through the boat's two masts with just inches to spare either side. The man operating the crane on the boat had such a fright that he fell overboard and broke a leg, dropping his load which crashed through the ship's deck. Jeremy was later arrested and prosecuted. Remarkably, he got off, pleading that he couldn't have taken any alternative route due to adverse weather conditions. This was characteristic for a man for whom normal rules didn't apply.

I was always pleased to see Jeremy as he, without fail, would liven things up. Once, however, when he was staying with me, I inadvertently livened things up for him. Jeremy had been out somewhere and I had had a young lady round to the flat. Later, I escorted her home but she was unable to get in because her husband had locked her out. There was no alternative but for her to stay with me. Next morning, I left for work early having arranged for a car to pick her up and take her home. Clearly, it would have been unseemly for a lady to be seen out in the morning in an evening dress and, as she left the flat, she grabbed an overcoat from the back of the door and put it on to avoid attracting attention on the street. When she reached home and took the coat off, her husband immediately snatched it from her and inspected it. He found the name 'Jeremy Bellville' in its collar. Unfortunately for Jeremy, this man knew him well as they were members of the same club. Incensed, he vowed to kill him. Prudently, Jeremy decided to leave the country for a while and lie low until the furore had died down. He saw the funny side of the incident and would never have sought to clear his name by dropping me in it. Our friendship wasn't tarnished in the slightest by the episode; indeed we had a good laugh about it next time we saw each other. I was always pleased to see him whenever he dropped in, usually unannounced.

Jeremy Bellville in typically ebullient mood (and a little too quick for the camera).

Jeremy was always up to something, but he was not the only one capable of high jinks. I remember one particularly memorable occasion at Belvoir Castle, the Leicestershire home of the Duke of Rutland, when I played a part in recommissioning part of that magnificent building's ancient defences. I had been invited to a dance by the Duke and, evidently, as the evening wore on we both became a little bored with proceedings. I don't recall which of us made the suggestion, but we went out onto the ramparts with the intention of finding out if we could get one of the castle's old cannons to fire. With no cannonballs to hand, the best we could come up with for ammunition were billiard balls. The Duke managed to find some powder and a fuse and we primed the cannon, struck a match and hoped for the best. Somewhat to our surprise, the cannon fired perfectly and the billiard ball flew out with some force. We hadn't been aiming for anything in particular, but the ball slammed into the side of the bus which had brought the band to the castle, causing, as one might expect, considerable damage. I'm sure the nature of the damage must have caused both the driver and the owner of the bus to scratch their heads.

All the while and on a rather more serious note, my career at Williams de Broë was blossoming. I tended towards corporate clients and institutions rather than private clients and must have been doing reasonably well because, in 1959, I was invited to become a partner. I knew the offer was imminent when I was given the key to the partners' lavatory shortly before receiving the news. At just twenty-five, I was the firm's youngest partner by some distance: Bob Williams, the next youngest was seventeen years older than me. My life during this period was great fun. I had many friends in London and I continued to enjoy the summer whirl of balls and parties. I would shoot during the autumn months and, as a guest of John Cowdray, shot grouse in Scotland for the first time. He was a fine sportsman despite having lost an arm at Dunkirk and, after the war, he was a prime mover in the revival of polo. He became a very dear friend with whom I would enjoy nearly fifty years of shooting and fishing, on his estates both in Scotland and in Sussex. We also shot together all over the country.

During the winters I began to acquire a taste for skiing and other winter sports, which, first the war and then, National Service had precluded me from taking up. I had first gone to Austria, though I can't recall to which resort, in the winter of 1957, during my second stint with the army. I was not a natural on skis and was put into a beginners' group with young children. I even struggled to come to terms with the T-bar lift which took us to the top of the slope, contriving to unseat a six year old boy I was travelling with. Next time, my exasperated instructor decided to travel up with me – he suffered the same fate. The following year I went to Switzerland, to St Moritz, keen to improve my skiing but, more importantly to test my mettle at the St Moritz Tobogganing Club (SMTC), or as it is more commonly known, the Cresta Run.

The SMTC was then very much a club for English gentlemen and I knew friends who had completed the run. It was through them that I was invited to have a go. Legend has it that, in its long history, the run has seen every bone in the human body broken, though mercifully it has claimed only four lives and is consequently statistically safer than playing marbles. The Cresta toboggan is ridden head first, face down and, unlike the skeleton used on other courses, it has neither steering nor brakes. The run itself was first built in 1885 and is rebuilt every winter to follow exactly the same course. It can only be used until mid-morning every day before the sun begins to melt the ice, making it too dangerous. Even in the fifties, before the development of aerodynamic helmets and skin tight Lycra, speeds at the bottom of the course reached 80 miles per hour: I wore shooting plus fours and an ordinary crash helmet. There are two starting points, 'top' and 'junction', the latter being about a third of the way down the course and opposite the club house. It was from here that I had my first exhilarating taste of tobogganing. It was enormous fun and I did rather well. Over three days, I rapidly improved. My first attempt was very slow, about 90 seconds; my second, a more respectable 60 seconds. Having found the right line on the run, I started to go much quicker. I completed my third run in 49 seconds, shaved a second off that time on my fourth attempt and then crossed the line in 47.4 on my fifth. This, fastest run, was within about two seconds of the course record at the time and I was determined to get even closer to that mark. Of course, the more weight on the toboggan, the greater the downhill momentum and the faster the speed. As I was quite light, I thought I could go faster if I added weight to my toboggan. Ignoring advice from a host of more experienced riders, including legendary Cresta champion, the Canadian Doug Connor, that modification would make the toboggan unstable, I had ten kilos of lead weights screwed to its underside. I should have listened. Though the weight did indeed increase my speed, it made the toboggan almost impossible to control. Like many before and since, I exited the track at the notorious Shuttlecock Corner, not the sharpest bend on the run but a long, low left hand bank designed to take the edge off a rider's speed about halfway down. If one is travelling too fast at Shuttlecock, one is certain to come off and it claims more victims than any other section of the course. Most, simply 'lip out' over the top of the bank and come to rest in soft snow or against bales of straw arranged to catch the errant. Not me. With my extra weight I arrived at Shuttlecock travelling much too quickly, perhaps 60 miles per hour, and out of control. I hit the bend, took off over its bank, and was still rising as I cleared the safety barriers. I eventually came to rest between the bank and some startled spectators and not far from some trees. Those who fail to get round the bend automatically become members of the Shuttlecock Club and are entitled to wear its tie. I have mine to this day. I would like to have improved on my best time of 47.4 and ought to have listened to those experienced riders who tried to warn me that it was folly to simply add weight to the toboggan in order to attempt to shave a few tenths of a second off. I wouldn't mind having one last go.

The year 1959 was a momentous one. Not only was I presented with the key to the partners' lavatory at Williams de Broë but it was also the year I married. I first met Marina Kennedy during the summer season of 1958 and we got to know one other better as we kept bumping into each other at various parties. She came from an interesting family. Her mother, Daška Ivanović-Banać, the daughter of a prominent politician, was born in Osijek in modern day Croatia and was considered one of Yugoslavia's great beauties, known locally as the Pearl of Dubrovnik. Her uncle, Ivan 'Vane' Ivanović, was educated at

Marina Kennedy, my first wife.

Westminster School and Peterhouse, Cambridge and was a great anglophile. He was a political activist and a director in the shipping company, Yugoslav Lloyd, owned by his elderly stepfather, Božo Banac. At the outbreak of World War II, acting on behalf of his ailing stepfather, Vane had made ten of the company's ships available to the British Ministry of War Transport. Later, in 1967, Prince Rainier III appointed Vane consul general of Monaco in London. Marina's parents had divorced when she was a child and she didn't see much of her father, Geoffrey Kennedy, though as I recall, I did visit him to ask for his daughter's hand.

I got on very well with Marina's stepfather, Neil 'Billy' McLean whom her mother married in 1949. He had served behind enemy lines during the war and had later become an MP for the Scottish Unionist Party, as the Scottish Conservatives were known until 1965. Outside public life, Billy led a very interesting life in the shady world of intelligence and some time later he would ask me to assist him with this work. I think Marina's family approved of me. Certainly our route to the altar was more conventional than that followed by her twin sister, Tessa. The

Into the Army

family had hit the headlines in 1957 when Tessa, aged just eighteen, eloped with Dominic Elwes, son of the portrait painter Simon Elwes. Dominic also painted but was not nearly as talented as his father; his best known work is a portrait of his friend, Lord 'Lucky' Lucan. The couple fled first to Scotland as Tessa's family took out an injunction against them marrying in England or Wales. They were hounded across the border by the media and decided to 'escape' to Havana where Castro's revolution was in full cry. They were married there, but shortly afterwards fled the growing violence aboard a raft with two *National Geographic* explorers, eventually making land at Miami. They went on to New York where, just to make sure, they were married again at Manhattan's Supreme Court. On their return to England, Elwes, whom I never much liked, spent a brief spell in Brixton prison and Tessa was made a ward of court.

In comparison to Elwes, I must have seemed a much safer son-in-law. Marina and I were married at St Mark's, North Audley Street, W1 and had our reception at the Dorchester before heading off for Monte Carlo on honeymoon. We were

Dressed for dinner.

both still quite young – Marina was just twenty and I was twenty-five, though I had certainly lived quite a full life in the seven years since I had left Eton. I had seen some of the world and the army had made a man of me and had been great fun. Through this period of my life I had maintained many of the great friendships that had been forged at school and added many more through the army and through life in the City. I had also made the most of London life as a bachelor for a number years. As the 1950s drew to a close, I was entering a new chapter of my life: I had begun a meaningful career in the City, was recently married and soon to become a father.

3. In the City and in the Country

Marina and I set up home together in a smart post-war terraced house in Hyde Park Square. Even though I had recently become a partner at Williams de Broë and was earning something in the region of £5,000 per year, a large house in such a fashionable part of London was beyond my means at this time. My uncle Sammy generously lent me £10,000 so that I could buy it: as I recall, it didn't take me terribly long to repay him. The house, well-located and spacious was ideal for raising a family and before long, our first child, a daughter, Daška Marina, arrived. She was born at Queen Charlotte's Hospital, Hammersmith and I went to see her just as soon as I could. I entered the hospital and asked a nurse if I could see my baby. She took me to a room which was full of screaming babies and I asked how on earth would I know which one was mine. 'Oh, she said, we tie a label to its cock.' 'That's no good to me', I replied, a little stunned. 'Mine's a daughter.' 'No', she said, 'COT!' I think she saw the funny side, and so did Daška when she was old enough to be told the story.

As things would turn out, we were not to remain long at Hyde Park Square and Daška was the only one of my children to have lived there. For the whole of the summer of 1961, I took a large house at Acrise, near Folkestone as a country retreat. I rented out our home in London and Marina and Daška spent the whole of the summer in Kent. In London, I rented a flat in Hays Mews near Berkeley Square which I used as a bolt hole during the week before heading south to spend the weekends with my young family. Such an arrangement was uncommon for the time and I suppose it has echoes of those very early days of my childhood when my family would all decamp to Brantridge during the summer months.

Acrise – Our home for the summer of 1961.

The eighteen weekends we spent at Acrise were great fun and we would always have friends to stay. We kept a guestbook which all those who visited signed and which I still have now: it bears some ninety or so signatures and scanning through them conjures some wonderful memories of the happy times we spent there. First to visit were my sisters, Clare (with her husband Peter) and Anne who would visit on two subsequent occasions. My father and his second wife Mary spent the Whitsun bank holiday with us and Sarah Henderson, my cousin with whom I had spent so much of childhood at Clarendon, also came with her husband Ian. My cousin, John, head of the family brewing business and, by that time, chairman of Ipswich Town FC, was another house guest, visiting in August. Among the friends who came for weekends were Mark Brocklehurst, a great friend of mine from school and from the City and Reggie Sheffield, the younger brother of Charlie who had perished in the fire at Shobrooke. The last guests to sign the book on the final weekend of August were my best man, Bryan Basset and his new wife, Carey, whom I always called my twin as she was born on exactly the same day as me. My mother-in-law would stay for longer periods during the week as company for Marina and to spend time with her granddaughter while I was in London.

One weekend, my dear friend from school, Jeremy Bellville visited. In typical Bellville style he turned up unannounced and uninvited though, as ever, I was delighted to see him and not totally surprised by his sudden appearance on my doorstep. I'm still not entirely sure how he knew we were there but, with Jeremy, you could never tell when he would turn up or how he would arrive. He was simply one of those characters who flitted in and out of one's life, enlivening it enormously through his energy and cavalier approach to life. Both his parents had money, so there was little need for him to work and he seemed to spend a good deal of time abroad, living it up. Whenever he decided to drop in we were always able pick up just where we had left off, no matter how long it had been since we had seen each other. At Acrise, Jeremy and I played croquet in front of the house till the early hours, the lawn floodlit by the headlights of our cars. The clunk of a croquet mallet striking a ball or that of a ball striking another are quintessentially English sounds: the spirit in which we played that night was revealed by a more tuneful sound, the clink of balls striking brandy glasses. It was enormous fun and I have no idea who won. I doubt either of us cared.

Always full of life and a risk-taker, Jeremy's luck ran out just a year later. In a very matter-of-fact way, *The Times*, on 22 August 1962, reported, 'A yachtsman, Mr Jeremy Bellville, aged 32, of Landford Lodge, Salisbury, Wiltshire, is presumed to have drowned in the river Yealm, near Newton Ferrers, Devon, after falling overboard from his motor yacht, the Charmaine, yesterday.' The truth of the matter was rather more in keeping with the way Jeremy lived his life. He had been with friends aboard the *Charmaine* (which didn't belong to him as *The Times* had reported), sipping champagne and cocktails when one of his guests decided to row ashore. As this friend set off, Jeremy shouted 'I'll race you!' and dived into the river in his dinner jacket. He was never seen again. He was so unpredictable that I and his other friends half expected him to turn up somewhere unannounced for some time afterwards. It wouldn't have been out of character for him to have waded ashore somewhere downstream and to have caught the London train soaking wet. As the days passed by, however, we eventually lost hope of ever seeing him again. He was great fun and had been a great friend; for as much as anything, I will remember him for the kindness he showed me when he took me under his wing on my first day at Eton.

Among my most vivid memories from Acrise were regular visits, perhaps every other weekend, to Le Touquet-Paris-Plage, one of France's most fashionable resorts where we would have lunch and then have some fun in the casino. On several occasions we took the 'air ferry' to Le Touquet, a scheduled service operated by Silver City Airways from Lydd Airport, just a few miles down the road from Acrise. Silver City flew Bristol Superfreighter aircraft which could carry about twenty passengers and three cars – we would always take one. On one particular weekend, we decided to make the journey to France under own steam. Among our guests was Vivyan Naylor-Leyland, a great friend and shooting companion. At this time, Vivyan was learning to fly and, under the tuition of a qualified pilot, he flew down to Kent from his home, Nantclwyd, in North Wales. The pilot was given the weekend off and Vivyan and I thought it would be a good idea to make use of his plane and fly over to France with my other weekend guests. I hadn't flown for some time, perhaps since my crash near Theale, and my private pilot's licence had expired whilst Vivyan was yet to earn his. Neither of these two facts deterred us, nor, it seems, unsettled our passengers and together we flew from Lympne Airport across to Le Touquet, returning that same evening. Fortunately, when we landed at Le Touquet's Côte d'Opale airport, neither Vivyan nor I were asked by the French authorities to produce documentary evidence to prove our credentials as pilots.

Throughout my life I have had a number of very fast cars. Whatever car I was behind the wheel of, whether the Ford Popular in which I had raced my friends to Marlow or the Ferrari I owned in the 1970s, I always liked to see how much I could get out of them. During the summer we were at Acrise, I briefly owned a unique car of some historical significance. I kept a car in London but needed another in Kent for getting to and from the railway station and for pottering about in. The car I chose was a Renault Dauphine, to all outward appearances a very sensible and rather unexciting family car. When *Road & Track* magazine road tested the Dauphine, it described its performance as 'peevish' with a top speed of just 80 mph and with acceleration from 0-60 mph taking a positively pedestrian 22.3 seconds. My Dauphine was a little different. Its meagre 845cc rear Renault engine had been replaced with a powerful Coventry Climax engine. The Coventry Climax was originally developed for fork lift trucks in the immediate post-war years but its impressive power to weight ratio began to draw interest from the motor racing fraternity. It was developed for racing and powered two Kieft 1100 cars at the Le Mans 24 hour race in 1954. It soon appeared in Formula 2 and then in Formula 1 in the back of chassis designed by John Cooper, the legendary racing car engineer. The Cooper-Climax team stormed to the Formula 1 championship in both 1959 and 1960 with Jack Brabham at the wheel. Away from the racetrack, Cooper experimented with production cars and before he found success with his Mini Cooper he dropped a Climax engine (though not the 2.5 litre Formula 1 version) into a Renault Dauphine. The Dauphine's engine compartment was at the rear of the car and it was consequently rear-wheel drive. Cooper soon realised that this created an imbalance which severely affected the handling of the car at speeds beyond which it was intended to travel. He gave up on the project and soon turned his attention to Alec Issigonis' revolutionary Mini, launched in 1959. The Mini's front-wheel drive was much better suited to Cooper's ambitions and the Mini Cooper remains one of the most iconic cars of its day and though the engines in the modern incarnation of the Mini are manufactured by BMW, sportier models still carry the 'Cooper' badge. In the summer of 1961, I became the owner of the only Renault Dauphine Cooper. I didn't know John Cooper but was aware of his work and snapped up the Dauphine when it became available. Its acceleration was frighteningly quick and on many occasions I raced away from traffic lights leaving seemingly much sportier vehicles in my wake. Once, I clocked more than 100 mph on a Kent beach. However, just as Cooper had discovered, I soon became aware that its handling was problematic and became dangerous at very high speeds as the poor weight distribution led its nose to rise: at full throttle it almost certainly would have taken off. Despite this obvious impracticality it was enormous fun to drive and I enjoyed seeing the startled looks of fellow drivers in my rear view mirror as I left them trailing. Later on, I would come to own many fast cars but few could match the raw power of that Dauphine even though its handling was about as stable as that of a Cresta Run toboggan weighed down with lead! Once we left Acrise and returned to Hyde Park Square, there was no need to keep the Dauphine as a 'run around' and I sold it on with something of a heavy heart.

Advertisement for a 1959 Renault Dauphine. With a Coventry Climax engine my model wasn't quite as family friendly. (Image courtesy of Alden Jewell)

All the while, I was working hard at Williams de Broë and it was from about this time that I began to make representations to my fellow partners that the company should merge with another City firm with a proud tradition, Panmure Gordon. I had many good friends at Panmure; Bryan Basset had been my best man and I had shared a flat with him for a while and there were others there with whom I had been friends since my school days. Another Old Etonian at Panmure at this time was Ian Cameron. Ian was two years ahead of me at school but we later became friends. He was great fun and, a year or so after I joined him at Panmure, I remember congratulating him on the birth of his third child: that child was a son named David who would grow up to become the prime minister. At a time when it was rare to move between firms in the City, Panmure invited me to join them. I declined but suggested that the two firms might merge as there was little overlap between the two businesses. Williams de Broë was strong in South Africa, on the Continent and in arbitrage, while Panmure Gordon specialised in corporate finance and new issue business. I recognised that the companies would fit well together but the other partners at Williams de Broë dismissed my suggestion for a merger without even giving it serious consideration. I would make similar representations on two further occasions and received the same response each time. I remember once, one of the older partners remarked, 'I've hung my hat on this peg for forty-seven years. If you think some whipper-snapper from Panmure is going to take it you're very much mistaken!' Throughout, Panmure remained very keen to take me on, and, when the suggestion for a merger was turned down a third time, I eventually felt able to accept their invitation.

In 1965, I joined them as market partner. Somewhat ironically, not long after I joined Panmure, Williams de Broë merged with another firm, Stanley.

In the interim, there had been other changes in my life. In 1963, my second daughter, Caroline Grace was born. Her second name was taken from one of her godmothers, Princess Grace of Monaco, known to millions of cinema-goers as the actress, Grace Kelly. Marina's grandmother, Milica, was great friends with Prince Pierre of Monaco and so it was that I found myself sitting next to his daughter-in-law, Princess Grace, for dinner while Marina and I were honeymooning in Monte Carlo. During the course of our stay we got to know Princess Grace and her husband, Prince Rainier, quite well.

Marina and I returned to Monte Carlo not long afterwards and spent more time with Prince Rainier and Princess Grace and I vividly remember playing croquet on the immaculate lawns of the Prince's Palace with the couple's young children, Caroline and Albert. Prince Pierre was an enthusiastic patron of the arts in Monaco and on one occasion he offered Marina and I two tickets for the opera. We had planned to go to St Tropez that day but we accepted the Prince's invitation and we took our seats just beneath the royal box in the Opéra de Monte Carlo for a production of Richard Wagner's *Tristan and Isolde*. Seldom could any stage production be blighted by such bad luck. Almost everything that could have gone wrong did go wrong. When a member of the cast was slapped on the back, his wig fell off and this and other calamities brought on an uncontrollable fit of the giggles in me. I was laughing so much that I had to be removed from the auditorium by Marina. When I saw the Prince afterwards he remarked with a wry smile that, from his vantage point above, he had noticed how much I had 'enjoyed' the performance. We arranged Caroline's christening to accommodate Princess Grace's busy schedule and her arrival in London for the ceremony at St Mark's, North Audley Street was kept a closely guarded secret. There was no media or public intrusion at all and it would be difficult to imagine such a high profile celebrity attending such an occasion today without the press or legions of fans getting wind of it.

The year before Caroline came along, we made the decision to move from Hyde Park Square after I spotted an opportunity too good to miss. I learned that three tumbledown three-storey townhouses in Seymour Walk, a cul-de-sac just off the Fulham Road, had come onto the market. The houses had suffered considerable bomb damage during the war and were in a dreadful state of repair, nothing having been done to them in the twenty or so years since. I saw that there was great potential to convert them into a very comfortable large house with a good sized garden and bought two of them for £7,500 each. I would have liked to have bought all three but was unable stretch that far. I engaged an architect and worked very closely with him in redeveloping the houses. Behind their elegant facades the interiors were practically gutted and I remember walking through one of the front doors and the whole house being open to the elements without any floors or roof. Work began and, where there had been two front doors there soon became one, where two staircases, one. The renovation work was expensive but certainly worth it. When it was completed, I had a large family home with seven bedrooms and five bathrooms; the top floor became a nursery and just as we had had at Clarendon, I installed a food lift. We took on a nanny and usually had one other lady in to cook or clean. Today, that part of London, SW10, is very fashionable indeed, but, at that time, my friends were somewhat bemused that I should choose to live so far out from the heart of the city, even though my new address was only two and a half miles west of where we had been living in Hyde Park Square. Some quipped that it was so far out of London that when they came to visit it felt like they were going to the races at Hurst Park.

In the short time that I had come to know him, I got on very well with Marina's stepfather, Billy McLean. Billy was one of those remarkable men who operated on the fringes of authority. During the Second World War he served in the Balkans and the Middle East with the Special Operations Executive (SOE), and he distinguished himself in Albania co-ordinating local resistance against the Nazis. He went there twice, accompanied on the second occasion by Major David Smiley and Captain Julian Amery who would both become long term associates: together, they acquired the epithet, 'The Musketeers'. In 1945, Billy was appointed military adviser to the British consulate at Kashgar, the remote city in western China which my Cobbold grandfather had first aimed for when he crossed the Karakoram watershed nearly half a century earlier.

Later, back in England, he pursued political ambitions and stood for the Conservatives in Preston South in 1950 and 1951. On both occasions he lost narrowly to Labour's Edward Shackleton (son of the Antarctic explorer): in 1951 the margin was a mere sixteen votes. He fared better next time around, winning Inverness for the Scottish Unionist Party (the Scottish

Conservatives) in a 1954 by-election. At that time, Inverness was, in geographical terms, the largest parliamentary constituency in Britain covering roughly four thousand square miles. Billy nursed the constituency well and the fact that he was, himself, a Highlander must have given him some credibility among the electorate. He held his seat at two subsequent general elections, in 1956 and 1959.

Of course, all this happened before I got to know Billy. Very quickly, I came to consider him as a friend and we spent a good deal of time together. We were both members of White's in St James's Street where we would often lunch together. I would also visit him at a house he took each summer near Inverness which was owned by another military maverick, Simon Fraser, Lord Lovat, whom I also knew quite well and who was a distant relative of my family. Consequently, in the autumn of 1964, when Billy asked me to help with his election campaign in Scotland, I had no hesitation in accepting. I arranged three weeks leave with Williams de Broë on the understanding that I would telephone the office every day to keep in touch and headed to Scotland to act as Billy's driver and mobile agent. Of course, finding a telephone box in the remote Highlands of Scotland was not always easy though I did manage to adhere to my daily commitment to ring the office. Together, Billy and I covered hundreds, if not thousands, of miles touring his remote constituency. My job was to make appointments for Billy to visit towns, make speeches and meet his constituents and then to ensure that he arrived on time and that everything ran smoothly. On my first day in this role, he was a little perturbed when I rolled up in an Alfa Romeo, which I owned at the time. His constituents were predominantly

Protestant and Billy expressed concern that an Italian car might provoke unhelpful associations with Rome and impair his chances of re-election. We decided not to take the chance and, whenever we arrived at a town where Billy was to make a speech or meet voters, we parked the Alfa well out of sight and completed our journey on foot.

Billy campaigned relentlessly. It was demanding work which had to run to a rigid schedule. The vast constituency included the Isle of Skye and we took the ferry from Mallaig on the mainland so that Billy could 'press the flesh' of the islanders. While there, we stayed in a well-known pub run by a jovial man named Campbell. On our last night on the island, I enjoyed his convivial hospitality to such a degree that I couldn't prise myself away from his bar to go to bed. The following morning, we left for the mainland and, bleary eyed, I had to drive Billy about two hundred miles for his next appointment: I didn't let on that I hadn't had a wink of sleep and that I'd had rather a lot to drink. Driving under the influence in those days was not frowned upon nearly as much as it rightly is today and I managed to both stay awake and to steer the Alfa around Scotland's twisting narrow roads.

Labour's candidate for Inverness at the 1964 election was also called McLean, Alexander Campbell, so we couldn't run on the slogan 'Vote McLean.' Instead, we plumped for 'Vote for the Right McLean' though as things would turn out neither Billy nor his namesake was returned to Parliament. I stayed with Billy in Inverness to witness the count as ballot boxes trickled in from all over the constituency. A recount was called but eventually Billy lost out to the Liberal, Russell Johnston, who secured a majority of just over two thousand. In the two years immediate to the election, Billy had not spent much time in the constituency and this, no doubt, caused his constituents to feel that he had neglected them, contributing to his defeat. Though many defeated MPs might rue the fact that they have lost touch with those to whom they owe their seat in the House of Commons, Billy's reasons for being away from his surgery in Inverness had nothing to do with complacency or neglect: the truth was altogether different. Whilst in public office he had continued to operate in the shady world of intelligence.

In the autumn of 1962, as the world held its breath for thirteen days after satellite images had revealed Soviet missile installations on Cuba, an escalating crisis in Yemen went almost unnoticed. The crisis followed the death of Imam (King) Ahmad and the succession of his son Mohamed al-Badr. Within a week of Ahmad's death, a group of army officers mounted a coup and declared Yemen a republic. Al-Badr escaped and fled to the mountains in the north of the country where he mustered support and formed a new royalist government. A civil war had begun. The republicans were backed by Nasser, Egypt's power-hungry president who, having seen off his country's former imperial masters during the Suez Crisis, now set his sights on the political domination of the Middle East. In this

A newspaper image of Mohamed al –Badr (centre).

ambition, Nasser was supported by the Soviet Union.

Billy, having been briefed on the crisis by King Hussein of Jordan, soon became an enthusiastic envoy for the royalists. Through shuttle diplomacy, he assembled an unlikely alliance against Nasser's grandiose schemes which included not only moderate Jordan and Saudi Arabia but also Israel. When the United States became the thirty-fourth country to recognise the new Yemen Arab Republic on 19 December 1962 it was Billy who persuaded the British foreign secretary, Lord Home and Prime Minister Harold Macmillan that they shouldn't follow suit. However, it soon became clear that the British government, embroiled as it was in scandal and becoming increasingly unpopular, would stop short of offering the royalists overt material support.

In March 1963, a course of action was discussed by five men at White's. Around the table that evening were Billy, Lord Home who, through Billy's reports, had remained sympathetic to the royalists' cause, minister for aviation, Julian Amery, one of Billy's fellow Musketeers from Albania, David Stirling, founder of the SAS and Brian Franks, the colonel commandant of the SAS. That this remarkable gathering determined to conduct a covert war, siding with the Yemeni royalists against a republican government which had been recognised by the United States and more than thirty other nations, is the stuff worthy of the most dramatic political thriller. Once a course of action had been decided upon, Home would have no further involvement, putting distance between the government and the operation lest anything should go wrong. This echoes my grandfather's mission to central Asia: though he was undoubtedly spying for the Government of

India, there was absolutely no documentary evidence to link him to his political masters should he encounter problems. After the meeting at White's, Lieutenant-Colonel Jim Johnson was approached to command the team of mercenaries, mostly SAS men, which would train and support the royalists on the ground. Johnson, a reservist, with 21 (Territorial) SAS, and a respected Lloyd's Underwriter chose David Smiley, the other Musketeer from Billy's second mission to Albania, as his second in command. Very little was known about the activities of these remarkable men until quite recently and the publication of a scholarly account of the conflict, T*he War that Never Was,* by Duff Hart-Davis.

In the three weeks I spent driving Billy through the beautiful scenery of the Scottish Highlands in the run up to the 1964 election, I had no idea that he had even been to the Yemen, let alone that he was actively supporting the royalists in a bloody civil war there. He certainly didn't give me any hint as such in the many hours we spent together at the time, though absolute discretion and the ability to keep one's mouth shut are of paramount importance in the sort of work he was engaged in. He must have seen similar qualities in me, for, a couple of years later, he would entrust me with a secret mission to the court of Imam al-Badr.

It was around this time that shooting began to play an increasingly important part in my life. I had always felt comfortable with a gun since I had first learned to handle one at Clarendon. During my childhood and throughout my life to this point I had shot fairly regularly. However, during my early adulthood, army life and the demands of forging a successful career had taken priority. I shot with John Cowdray on his

Scottish and English estates every year from 1956 until his death in 1995 and I owe him a great deal. Through my friendship with him, I met many other keen sportsmen and received invitations to shoot all over the country and, occasionally, overseas. During the sixties, having established myself in the City and now earning a good living, I was able to indulge my love of field sport much more often, spending time with old friends and making many new ones along the way.

I logged my shooting activities in a series of game books which record where I shot, with whom, the weather conditions and the numbers of birds and other wildlife shot. I also pasted in many photographs which bring back happy memories spent in the company of great friends and interesting acquaintances. I was fortunate enough to stay in some of the country's finest stately homes, wonderful places to relax between shoots and set in beautiful countryside. I shot grouse from Wentworth Woodhouse the Yorkshire home of the Fitzwilliams and the largest private house in Britain which boasts the longest façade of any country house in Europe. The Fitzwilliams have been very dear friends

Wentworth Woodhouse. The façade is so long it wouldn't fit on one photograph.

for a very long time and have always shown me great kindness: Tom, the 10th Earl, and his charming wife, Joyce, in particular. They were much older than me and in many respects treated me as a son. When, in 1963, I was ill with pancreatitis, they insisted that I recuperate at Milton, their home near Peterborough: Marina and I stayed for three weeks and they showed us enormous kindness. Though neither Tom nor Joyce are still with us, my friendship with the family endures to this day.

I shot frequently, as well, with the Manton family at Houghton, and Mimi Manton is godmother to my son, Robert, though she protested at being asked, insisting she would be too old by the time he needed her. She couldn't have been more wrong. Still very sprightly at ninety, she has been a marvellous godmother, once hilariously hollowing out a Tattersalls racing book to secrete illicit sweets and posting the contraband to Robert at Ludgrove. The school took a very dim view of this prank, which naturally increased our delight.

I was also a regular guest at Blenheim Palace, at Wynyard in County Durham, at Normanby, the Lincolnshire home of the Sheffields, at Dixton in Gloucestershire and at Haddon Hall, on the Atholl estates of central Scotland and, of course, on John Cowdray's estates in Aberdeenshire and in West Sussex.

Aside from work and family, almost all of my time from the early sixties onwards became taken up with shooting and I would travel prodigious distances to accept invitations. Often, Marina would come with me, though the girls seldom joined us, remaining in London with their nanny. Scarcely a weekend would pass between the Glorious Twelfth and the following spring when I wouldn't be off somewhere to shoot. A typical day would begin quite early after a hearty breakfast. If we were shooting grouse in the summer and the weather was fine we would take lunch on the moors where our wives and girlfriends might join us. Through the autumn and winter when we shot pheasants or if the weather was not so good we would return to the house for lunch before going out again in the afternoon. We would generally call it a day at about four and take drinks back at the house and perhaps play bridge for a while, before getting ready for dinner which was often quite a sumptuous affair.

My game books record some memorable days' shooting. In December 1965, I was shooting at Wynyard with Lord Londonderry when a post-war record was set for the estate. Between eight of us, on the Home Beat, we shot 479 partridges in a single day, 360 of them before lunch. I recorded, 'Drew terribly well at No. 4 and had shooting every drive.' For good measure, we also shot three hares, three teal, fourteen duck and five pigeons. Among my companions that day were my friends Robin and David McEwen, two of the six sons of Sir John McEwen, who had served as lord of the treasury in Churchill's wartime government. That Wynyard record stood for exactly two years and I was among those who broke it. I was with a party which included my great friend, Mark Brocklehurst, which bagged 565 pheasants, despite our being delayed by early morning fog. Again, I shot at number four and, again, I reached a century before lunch. I kept my game card as a souvenir of our success though the number of birds killed is only one part of what makes an agreeable day's shooting. Most important is the camaraderie of one's companions which can make even a frustratingly unsuccessful shoot a very enjoyable day.

Conditions that day were ideal, at least they were once the fog had lifted. Whether it is a sunny day, raining or even snowing, it is the strength and direction of the wind which is most important to a successful shoot. Birds tend to fly downwind and just below the wind; therefore, if the wind is strong they will fly low, sometimes not much higher than head height. This doesn't present much of a challenge and makes for a rather dull shoot: far better to have them high and curling. A lot of preparation would go into a day's shooting and gamekeepers and beaters played an important part in determining the success of the day. Most head keepers knew exactly what was required of them but on the odd occasion poor decisions could ruin a day. One of my game books records one such occasion. In October 1964, having had a disappointing day, I wrote, 'Quite a lot of partridges but day was ruined by 'x' [name withheld] who is quite the stupidest and most obstinate keeper I have ever met. Out of seven drives, we had five upwind, one crosswind and one downwind which was a failure as he tried to drive 50 acres of sugar beet across the furrow without dogs.' Very occasionally, one's day might also be spoiled by one's companions. Etiquette has it that each gun only shoots at what is

Out shooting.

in front of him. Clearly, some draws are better than others and those with a particularly competitive nature are simply unable to resist shooting across their own draw to steal birds from their neighbours. I never descended to such tactics, relying on the luck of the draw and concentrating only on what flew in front of me. I always saw a day's shooting as a collaborative effort among friends rather than a competition between rivals. I have to say, that with only a very few exceptions, those I shot with were of the same mind.

As in any sport, one not only has good days but also bad days when one is out of touch. Often, a loss of form is inexplicable and the frustration it brings contrives only to make matters worse: the more one tries to put things right, the worse the form becomes. For a few days in November 1964, I was like a batsman struggling to put bat on ball or a tennis player unable to land a first serve. On a wet day at Wynyard, I got off to a reasonable start, shooting the first nine birds in front of me. Then, mystifyingly, I lost my form altogether and was unable to hit anything at all. I wrote in my game book, 'I have shot pheasants badly all year but nothing like this.' Things improved marginally the following day though I still suffered 'some inexplicable lapses' and was completely unable 'to hit anything coming straight towards me.' I concluded that I must have been checking during the swing, but like a golfer with the 'yips' I was unable to correct things and I became quite disheartened. The problem persisted. A couple of days later, at New England, near Newmarket, I again shot badly, still unable to hit a straight bird and the realisation dawned on me that there was 'something seriously wrong, not just an off day.'

Thankfully, my form improved a few days later 'after a visit to the shooting school' while at Tulliemet in Perthshire with the Duke of Atholl. We broke the Tulliemet record and I certainly shot much better than I had for some time and even killed my first blackcock, a large and rare cousin of the red grouse. Things got even better the following day, when, just down the road at Dunkeld, we shot no fewer than sixteen capercaillie. The capercaillie is the largest member of the grouse family and males can grow up to 35 inches long with a wing span of up to 50 inches and are renowned for their strutting mating displays. They were quite a rare sight then and I wouldn't be at all surprised if the sixteen we bagged that day was a world record. Today, they are extremely rare and enjoy protected species status. A statue of a strutting male in my garden reminds me of our success that day.

'More birds than I have ever seen' was the entry I made in my game book on 11 November 1965. I was at Westwood, the Earl of Dudley's estate at King's Langley north of London, shooting with the Earl's sons, and also with the Duke of Marlborough, Lord Bruntisfield and with Hugh Fraser, the younger brother of Simon 'Shimi' Fraser, 15th Lord Lovat. It was one of the most memorable day's shooting I have ever had; in all, we shot 750 pheasants, a staggering 650 of these before lunch. We also bagged a woodcock, two partridges, four hares and twenty wild duck. The tally was a record for Westwood. I shot again with the Duke of Marlborough a few weeks later at Blenheim over New Year when we had two marvellous days, the second of which I described in my log book as 'The best day's shooting I have ever had.' We had six drives in all, the first standing on Blenheim's famous bridge and the last across its beautiful lake.

There was a strong wind and I described the birds as being 'very high and curling.'

I always looked forward enormously to my visits to Dunecht, the Scottish home of John Cowdray. John was the most generous host and his seven estates offered excellent sport over more than 50,000 acres of wonderful Scottish countryside. I would make several visits each year, shooting grouse in the late summer and early autumn, pheasants through the winter and occasionally spending Easter with him while taking in some salmon fishing on the Dee which flows through the estates. I enjoyed countless memorable days' sport in these wonderful surroundings. Among them, during an extended stay in September 1964, I saw more grouse than I had ever seen on John's Edinglassie estate. Despite bad weather, we killed more than 800 birds over five days. This figure might have been even higher but for bad weather. I noted in my game book that 'We might easily have got 200 brace each day with better weather and a better team of guns. Unfortunately John C. had hurt his arm and cannot shoot all year.' The following spring, during another visit, Marina caught her very first salmon, weighing in at a healthy nineteen pounds. I have many fond memories of my time at Dunecht, but one odd incident sticks in my mind especially. I was shooting a drive called Hill of Fare with John's regular loader loading for me. As I recall, my loader was with John elsewhere in the drive, organising a shoot for the following day. All of a sudden, a pair of roe deer appeared, prancing across the grouse moor. We kept very still, and I whispered to the loader, 'What would his Lordship do?' The loader replied without hesitation that his master would shoot them. He handed me my gun and I killed them both. When I returned to the house later, John very much approved of what I had done.

On another occasion I was staying at Dunecht for the first day of the salmon fishing season, always 1 February on the Dee. At 8 o'clock in the morning, John came to my room and informed me that I wouldn't be able to fish because there were ice floes the size of piano tops flowing down the river. He told me that he had arranged for me to go shooting instead and, after breakfast, I went out as the only gun with three keepers and six beaters. Three or four hours later, I returned to the house for lunch and told John that I'd had rather a good morning, shooting forty-five cock pheasants. He had some good news too: the river had thawed and I would be able to fish in the afternoon. I landed two salmon, rounding off a thoroughly enjoyable and memorable day.

Dunecht, the Scottish home of John Cowdray.

Not far from Dunecht, I also shot at Beauly, the family seat of the Lovats. Shimi, as his colourful war career might suggest, was full of mischief and apt to playing practical jokes. On one occasion I remember being the butt of one of these. On this particular day, the pheasants on his estate were flying across the

Beauly River, out of sight from dry land. Shimi suggested I take to the river in order to have a go at them, a suggestion which seemed eminently sensible until I saw the size of the boat he would have me board. It was about the size of a small table and evidently so unstable that his only motive must have been to witness me fall in to the cold, clear waters of the river. Undeterred and always ready for a challenge, I got in gingerly and pushed off from the bank, keeping as low as possible in order to keep the boat as stable as I could. Whenever I saw a pheasant I raised myself up on to my knees in order to get a shot off before getting low again. There was absolutely no question of standing up to shoot and in this way I managed to kill two or three birds, Shimi standing on the bank laughing all the while. I'm glad to say I didn't give him the satisfaction of falling in.

I always enjoyed shooting abroad and was fortunate to be invited to Spain by my friend, Dru Montagu, who lived there, on several occasions. I first went in October 1964 and enjoyed the experience greatly. It was very different to the sport I was used to in Britain; we rode on horseback high into the hills on successive partridge drives and we each had a Spanish loader and two secretarios, 'pickers up' whose job it was to retrieve what we had shot – there were no dogs. These men were very eager in their task and were inclined to seize the next gun's birds in order to outdo their competitors alongside them. The last of the three days I spent there was particularly memorable. Between eight of us we probably killed 350 brace and this figure might have been higher had a pair of eagles not turned a lot of birds back in the first drive. In the afternoon we stood in a deep ravine between two cliffs with the birds flying straight across, some 120 feet high. The secretarios were not as good at retrieving birds as dogs might have been and many were lost in the river or under boulders.

Among other places I shot regularly was Dumbleton in Gloucestershire, the estate of the Hambro family; I was good friends with Charlie Hambro whose mother was Pamela Cobbold, youngest daughter of John Dupuis Cobbold, my great uncle. Invariably, Ian Coley would load for me at Dumbleton. Ian, himself a first rate shot, was kind to nominate me for *Field* magazine's top 100. He has coached the British Olympic team on no fewer than six occasions. Nantclwyd in Denbighshire, the home of Vivyan Naylor-Leyland, my co-pilot on that flight to Le Touquet, was another of my regular haunts, as was Marchmont in Berwickshire, the home of the McEwens. In my native Wiltshire, I would shoot at Wilton with Lord Pembroke, whom I had known since my childhood days at Clarendon and who named a wood on his estate 'Cobbold's Wood' after I had shot there. I'm not sure if it still bears my name. Of course, I always looked forward to shooting at Clarendon, by this time in the hands of my uncle, Sammy. It was as if I knew every inch of its five thousand acres and each visit brought back

At Dumbleton. Ian Coley is loading for me.

vivid memories of my adventurous childhood there.

When Sammy returned from the war and married, my grandmother moved out of Clarendon and made her home a short distance away at Ashley Hill, a house she and my grandfather had built many years earlier. I remained very close to her and would always find time to visit her. I felt a great sense of loss when she died on 5 November 1966, just a few weeks short of her eighty-ninth birthday. She was laid to rest in the grounds of her beloved Clarendon in consecrated ground atop a hill: if the estate were still in the hands of my family, this is where I would ask to be buried, in the soil of the place I have always considered home and alongside the remarkable woman who played such an important role in my upbringing and whom I loved dearly. Sadly, Sammy died just two years after my grandmother, in 1968, and Clarendon passed to my cousin, Andrew Christie-Miller. It remained in his care until 2006 when it was sold outside the family.

The year before my grandmother died, my third daughter, Arabella was born. In that same year, 1965, I lost my Cobbold grandfather, Ralph, at the grand old age of ninety-six. Some time earlier, he suffered a nasty fall at his home in Cornwall. He had got up to let his dogs out and had fallen down the stairs to Penrice's cellars, where he had lain undiscovered for some hours with several cracked ribs and other injuries. Already well into his nineties, it was an accident from which he never fully recovered. He spent his last days in hospital in London and I remember visiting him there. I also attended his funeral at Golders Green crematorium from where my father conveyed his ashes to Trimley in Suffolk where they were interred. My father later confessed that he had somehow contrived to leave the urn on the train he took to Suffolk though, thankfully, he had managed to retrieve them. In many ways, my grandfather remained something of a mystery to me even after his death. I had never got to know him terribly well and he was reticent about his adventures in central Asia, Abyssinia and during the Great War. Only recently, have I become fully aware of his extraordinary adventures. A man of enormous pluck, the missions he undertook are worthy of any great imperial ripping yarn and his exploits continue to intrigue and engross historians of Britain's imperial heyday.

Not long after my grandfather died, I was asked to undertake my own secret mission. Though nothing like as dangerous as the assignments Ralph had taken on, it was potentially quite risky and required maximum discretion. In Billy's cause to repel the Nasser-sponsored republicans from Yemen, his greatest challenges were to maintain the support of other Middle Eastern states for the royalist cause and to secure the means which would enable the royalists to sustain their campaign. The Yemeni royalists needed two things – training and cash. The former would come from small teams of British mercenaries recruited and led by Johnson and Smiley, the latter from the rulers of sympathetic neighbours. The revolution and al-Badr's subsequent flight from Sana'a had cut the king off from his considerable financial resources. It was clear that if he were to have any hope of overturning the revolution and expelling Nasser's troops, he would need the resources with which to buy weapons and secure the support of tribal chiefs. This is where I came in.

I would lunch quite regularly with Billy at White's where the flow of our conversation might typically cover family, business, sport or politics. Not once in all the time that I had known him had he divulged any details of his intelligence work. All that changed one day. I am not exactly sure when this meeting took place, but I know that I was at Panmure Gordon and that it occurred before the British mercenaries withdrew from Yemen – suggesting that it was probably 1966. I knew of Billy's history in covert operations and I had an inkling that he was still involved in work of a secret nature; it therefore didn't come as a complete shock when he asked for my help. The request was simple: would I consider taking a substantial quantity of gold from Saudi Arabia to the Yemeni royalists? It was a proposal the grandson of Ralph Patteson Cobbold was never likely to turn down and I told Billy there and then that I would be glad to help.

As in all Billy's dealings in relation to the civil war in Yemen, the requirement for secrecy was paramount. My mission would involve spending some weeks in the Middle East and I would have to do this without telling anyone the nature of my mission. I quite enjoyed this element of my task and, fortunately, my career in the City offered me a plausible explanation for my absence. I simply told Panmure that I needed to travel to the Middle East on business and that I may be away some time. I spun the same story to Marina who had absolutely no reason to suspect that I was up to anything else. Within a few weeks and at my own expense I boarded a flight for Jeddah.

When I arrived, I was met by a man called Zaid Sudairi, an adviser to King Faisal in the capacity of something akin to aide-de-camp, whose family was closely connected to the Saudi royals. I was very well looked after as arrangements were made for me to cross the border into Yemen. It was proposed that I make the journey either by jeep or by camel and that I would be accompanied by twenty or so men. I was to travel in full Arab garb, including headdress, and I was measured for and fitted with a fine set of robes which I still have to this day. I had been in Saudi Arabia for about a fortnight when David Smiley arrived. Smiley, who had been in from the start, had become field commander of the mercenary force in 1965 and operational decisions concerning the deployment of British soldiers in Yemen were made by him. When I met him, he advised me that the time was not right for my mission and that I was to be stood down. I was terribly disappointed but simply had to accept the judgment of a man who was as familiar with the strategic situation in the country as anyone. Having prepared myself mentally and physically for the mission, there was nothing for it but to head back to London wondering what might have been. Though I never got to set foot in war-torn Yemen, it was still quite an experience. Above all, I was pleased that Billy had felt able to take me into his confidence and thought me suitable to help him. The details of covert British involvement on behalf of the Yemeni royals have only recently come to light; for many years I remained tight-lipped about my small involvement to friends and family alike.

In 1967, Nasser pulled Egyptian troops out of the Yemen and the British mercenary force also withdrew. The war petered out and, in 1970, Saudi Arabia recognised the Yemen Arab Republic. Royalist supporters, with the exception of al-Badr's family, were integrated into the new regime. In 1990, the YAR and the People's Democratic Republic of Yemen, which had evolved from the former British colony of Aden and the

Protectorate of South Arabia, were unified as the Republic of Yemen.

I kept in touch with Zaid Sudairi who had been my obliging host during my stay in Saudi Arabia. I remember some time later he visited me in England and I took him to the races at Newbury. There, he demonstrated an eye for a horse, so common among his countrymen. As the horses were parading, one caught Zaid's eye and he turned to me and confidently asserted that it was the one to back, despite it being unfancied in the betting. Sure enough, the horse won at a canter, barely coming off the bridle. Some years after my aborted mission, I returned to Saudi Arabia to visit Zaid. He took me far into the desert to meet his father, an influential man who had never been abroad. His camp was just as one might imagine an opulent desert dwelling and I was extremely well looked after. I spent a very comfortable ten days or so there and, each day, we would venture out into the desert to hunt for bustard with saker falcons and for hares

Hunting in the Arabian desert with saker falcons.

and desert foxes with salukis, Arabian greyhounds. The falcons were majestic birds and when not being used they would be tethered to posts outside our tents. Zaid's father was most generous in his hospitality; this even extended to passing truck drivers who would be invited into the camp to be fed and watered. Among the other guests staying with Zaid's father was Salem bin Laden. Salem and I became great friends, often meeting up whenever he was in London. He died in 1988 when the light aircraft he was piloting hit power lines near San Antonio; this long before his young half-brother achieved international notoriety. I enjoyed my holiday in the desert immensely. I remember washing in a nearby river and, for the first time in my life, I grew a moustache. This caused great amusement to my children when I returned home. They insisted I shave it off immediately.

Not long after I returned from Saudi Arabia and my aborted mission to Yemen, Marina and I decided to separate and then divorce. No great drama prompted this decision and there was certainly no other party involved; it simply seemed that with so much going on in my life we had gradually drifted apart. The separation was very amicable and we put the needs of the girls first. I stayed in Seymour Walk while Marina moved not far away with the girls, whom I continued to see as much as I could. It is never easy for children when their parents separate but I hope that the sensible and grown up way in which we handled our divorce helped them through this period of upheaval. Marina and I have remained friends ever since.

For a few years, I reverted to the life of a bachelor, while I continued to enjoy my life in the City with Panmure Gordon. Shooting continued to play a very large part in my life and, as the seventies dawned, I came up with a novel idea to cut down the number of hours I spent travelling to pursue my passion for it.

4. To the Skies

I adjusted back to life as a single man relatively quickly. Those most dear to me, my three daughters, remained nearby and Marina did nothing whatsoever to impede my access to them. My work at Panmure Gordon continued to consume my attention during the week and shooting and the fellowship of my many close friends ensured that I was seldom lacking in company away from the office. I was not to re-marry until late in 1970 and though it might be slightly misleading to suggest that I played the field in the interim, I was not particularly lacking in female company either.

The one enduring relationship I had during this period was with a French girl, named Brigitte. It was through her that I became the guest, for the second time in my life, of the Rothschilds. Brigitte was a great friend of Baron Guy de Rothschild, the cousin of Philippe who had looked after me so well during my visit to the Bordeaux region as a young man. In October 1967, I received an invitation from Baron Guy to shoot at Château de Ferrières, his residence near Paris. Among the baron's other guests were Prince Alfonso Hohenlohe, a very colourful man who was the driving force behind the development of Marbella and the Costa del Sol and Georges Pompidou who, a year later, would be elected president of France. I got on very well with Pompidou and met him on a few further occasions, and remember having one particularly memorable evening with him and a couple of girls at Annabel's when he visited London once. The evening was enormous fun: rather more fun I suspect than that which had been scheduled in his official itinerary. He had been due to have dinner with the British foreign secretary, George Brown, but cancelled that engagement at No. 11 for something a little more lively with me at Annabel's. The day I spent at Ferrières was very hot and windless for the time of year and I saw more pheasants that day than I think I have ever seen. Together, we killed 871 and on one drive alone I shot between 75 and 100. I was on particularly good form and I must have shot a third of the total killed; there were so many pheasants that I even killed two birds with a single shot. I returned to Ferrières on Boxing Day of the same year and then again in October 1968 when we shot even more pheasants. From there, I flew to Morocco, to another Rothschild house, where I spent a couple of very enjoyable days shooting snipe and hunting wild boar.

Baron Guy de Rothschild and Georges Pompidou at Ferrières.

To the Skies

Once when I was at Ferrières, Henry Cotton, three-time winner of the Open Golf Championship, was staying there too. On the Sunday after shooting, I made up a three with Guy and Henry on a course which Henry had designed in the late 1930s but had never played or even seen due to the intervention of the war. It was the most cleverly designed course with only three greens. Eighteen ingeniously positioned tee positions, however, enabled one to play eighteen holes. Though in his sixties, Henry could still play a bit and he was very good company. We became friends and I played with him again, later, in the Algarve where, instead of having a caddy, he employed a donkey to carry his clubs around the course.

Since my adventures on the Cresta Run, I hadn't been to the Alps much. I was never a natural on skis – I could go fast in a straight line but my turns left a little to be desired and I seldom made coming to a halt look effortless. Undaunted by this distinct lack of natural ability, I returned to the Alps in the late sixties. On this occasion I went to Cortina, Italy's most stylish winter resort. I travelled with two close friends, Johnny Louden and Alexander McEwen and we decided it would be fun to drive down through Europe. At that time I had a Bentley and, having reached the Continent, we took turns at the wheel and made it to Cortina in good time. I hadn't let on to anyone, but there was to be more to this particular holiday than just skiing with some good friends. For a short time I had been seeing a young lady in London and together we made secret plans to meet up in Cortina. Travelling independently, she was to work in the resort, looking after somebody's children or perhaps teaching English – I can't remember exactly. When she was not working, I would excuse myself from my friends and go to see her at the house of her employers. Though we had intended to keep our meetings secret, I had not thought things through well enough and our tryst was undone. The problem was my car. It was the only Bentley in Cortina at the time and it was very distinctive: certainly distinctive enough to betray my whereabouts to anyone who knew me when it was parked up outside my girlfriend's place. I took a little ribbing.

If the Bentley was something of a liability while I was in Cortina, it came into its own on the journey back. On New Year's Day (I can't be entirely sure which year, but perhaps 1968), I hosted a dinner party for some seventy or eighty friends, even though I had a Channel ferry to catch the following day. The evening was very enjoyable and, reluctant to abandon my guests, I stayed as long as I dared, all the while making mental calculations of how long it would take me to get to Ostend. Eventually, I tore myself away from the party at about 11 o'clock and Alexander and I sped off in the Bentley. Our ferry would depart in something like nine or ten hours and we had over 700 miles to cover through Italy, Austria, West Germany and Belgium. Fortunately, there was very little else on the roads, which once through the Alps were straight and fast. We floored the Bentley and ate up the miles at an average speed, excluding stops, of well over 100 miles per hour. We made the Belgian coast in time to catch our ferry home.

A fast, comfortable, reliable car was precisely what I needed to get me all over the country to shoot. From the Home Counties to the Highlands, from north Wales to East Anglia, I drove thousands of miles every year in pursuit of sport, spending many hours at the wheel every week during the shooting seasons. As a young man, one doesn't give a second thought to driving such prodigious distances, particularly in the pursuit of one's passion. However, later in life such a punishing schedule begins to take its toll and as I reached my seventies I increasingly found it difficult to accept all of the invitations I received. Much earlier, for a few years during the early 1970s, I was able to reduce my travelling time around the country and abroad to a fraction of what it had been before or was thereafter. For the second time in my life I took to the skies.

After my narrow escape in a field in Theale on my twenty-second birthday, I hadn't flown at all apart from that trip with my guests at Acrise to Le Touquet. The exhilaration and sense of freedom which flying affords, however, never quite leaves one and in my mid-thirties I began to take flying lessons again. This was not to regain my private pilot's licence so that I could fly aeroplanes again: rather, I chose to learn how to fly helicopters. I had been up in someone else's helicopter and had been riveted by it and I remember thinking that this was for me. In 1969, I took lessons at Kidlington, near Oxford, and spent a series of weekends there accumulating the minimum thirty flying hours needed in order to gain a helicopter licence. As the airfield was near Blenheim, the Duke of Marlborough, known to his friends as Bert, very kindly offered to put me up for several weekends in a row. I would travel down from London after work on Friday, and stay all weekend, driving the short distance between Blenheim and Kidlington on both Saturday and Sunday for lessons. Bert was a great friend with a lightning wit. Once, at Blenheim (though I wasn't staying at the time), one of his guests, an American lady, lit up a cigarette at dinner. This wasn't quite the done thing even in those days and Bert let the lady know that he was most unimpressed. In response to his complaint, the lady said, 'But Bert, nothing gives me greater pleasure.' Without a moment's hesitation, Bert riposted, 'nothing gives me greater pleasure than fucking, but I don't do it between the soup and the fish!'

One year, I was staying at Blenheim for Whitsun and we were having lunch on the Bank Holiday Monday. Everyone who knew Bert well knew that on Mondays he went 'walking out' with a lady friend when he was supposed to be out farming. Bert believed these liaisons were a closely guarded secret but we all knew about them. This girlfriend had joined us for lunch, and was an appropriate distance down the table from Bert. Halfway through lunch Bert sneezed and then remarked that he thought he had hay fever. 'I don't suppose Emily (not her real name) has been wearing a grass skirt?' I remarked. Everyone around the table roared with laughter with the exception of Emily herself and, of course, Bert whose face didn't betray the slightest emotion. It was an audacious remark

The 10th Duke of Marlborough – 'Bert' to his friends.

for one as young as I was to make to such a distinguished host but indicative, I suppose, of how at home I felt at Blenheim.

Bert had a chauffeur-valet named Bramwell, who went almost everywhere with him. Bramwell liked a drink, not the best proclivity for someone whose primary role involved driving, but Bert was very attached to him. There are enough stories about Bramwell to fill a book, but there are a couple at which I was present. Once, I was staying with Bert in Jamaica and we'd been playing bridge. Bramwell came in at about 7 o'clock, clearly the worse for wear, picked a score sheet up from the table, screwed it up and nonchalantly tossed it out of the back of his hand towards the waste paper basket. His throw missed. 'Pick it up, Bramwell!' barked Bert. 'No I won't, Bertie!' came the impertinent reply. 'Bramwell, you're drunk!' Bertie continued. 'You're drunk, too, Bertie!' said Bramwell. In no time at all they were squaring up to one another. This was a rather comical scene, because Bert at 6'4" was a good foot taller than Bramwell. Before fists started flying, I was able to come between them and sent Bramwell to his room.

On another occasion, we'd been to Biarritz and were boarding the plane home. As Bert and I ascended the steps, I noticed that Bramwell was nowhere to be seen. I looked over to the airport buildings and, to my astonishment, Bramwell was there waving us goodbye from the top of the stand. I went off to get him and found that he was blind drunk and determined not to get on the plane. With some difficulty, I managed to get him on board and he spent the entire flight sipping from a brandy flask. When we landed, we went our separate ways and I can only imagine how Bramwell managed to drive all the way back to Blenheim. The unusual relationship between Bert and Bramwell was quite moving in many ways. Not long after Bert's death in 1972, I was shooting at Blenheim and Bramwell approached me asking if he could load for me. I was touched as it was clear that he was finding it difficult to come to terms with the loss of Bert. He said to me, 'I do miss the old boy.'

When I started learning to fly a helicopter, I'd had no means of getting one of my own, and, once qualified, I intended to hire one out for use at weekends. Some time into my training, however, I had a coup in the City. A contact in Australia urged me to buy shares in a mining company, Poseidon NL. In September 1969, Poseidon had discovered a promising site for nickel, a metal which at that time was in great demand due to the Vietnam War. On my contact's advice I bought 3,000 shares in Poseidon at about £2 each. When Poseidon struck nickel in a big way, the company's share price soared to £125 almost overnight, turning a holding worth £6,000 into one of over £350,000. Unfortunately, I was unable to capitalise fully on what became known as the 'Poseidon bubble.' At that time capital gains tax was 98.75% and selling the shares would have entirely wiped out my profit. Instead, I took a loan of £75,000 against the value of the shares in order to buy my first helicopter. On 29 March, Easter Sunday, 1970, I took my three daughters to Battersea heliport to take delivery of G-AXXO (XO for short), the call sign of my new helicopter. XO was a Bell 206 JetRanger, a sophisticated American model which became the definitive helicopter for corporate use for more than thirty years. It accommodated five with comfort, two upfront and three across a bench seat in the rear, just like a good-sized family saloon car. It arrived from the States in kit form and I would often visit Alan Mann Helicopters in Woking to

To the Skies 125

see how its assembly was coming on. I was itching to take it up and, that Sunday, not even a serious skiing injury could keep me from taking the controls. Precisely a week earlier, I had fallen at speed while at Klosters, breaking my leg in ten places. The break was too complicated to put into plaster and my leg had been put back together with seventeen pins and nails and a bar down the front of my shin. It was thought that I would need to spend three weeks in hospital in Switzerland, but I managed to persuade my surgeon that I could go home, assuring him that I would have both a day nurse and a night nurse to look after me. I was on crutches for many weeks afterwards during which I was unable to drive a car; fortunately the foot controls of a helicopter require only the lightest touch and my injury simply wasn't going to delay my maiden flight in XO.

At this time, I hadn't quite accumulated enough hours to

Taking delivery of G-AXXO with my daughters.

fly solo and on that first flight I was accompanied by John Dickin, Charlie Hambro's pilot. Also with us was Susie McKinley Wilson. Susie and I had met in London about a year earlier and had walked out together briefly before she went home to Melbourne. When she returned to England a year later, she telephoned me and we started seeing each other regularly; we married in late October, 1970. We all took off from Battersea at 11:20 a.m. We flew first to Chicheley Hall near Newport Pagnell to have drinks with my friend, David Beatty and his family and, from there, we headed west to Cirencester for lunch with Michael Naylor-Leyland. After a stop to re-fuel at Staverton Airport near Gloucester we went to the Bathurst estate for an Easter egg hunt. We landed back at Battersea at 17:45 having packed a lot into the day.

Susie McKinley Wilson, my second wife.

The long Easter weekend afforded another chance to get up in the air and we all returned to Battersea the following morning, Easter Monday. We were off for lunch with my sister Anne and her husband, Tom Egerton, at their home in Mountfield, Sussex. Not long into the flight, it became apparent that XO had a minor fuel leak and I thought it prudent to get down as soon as possible. We radioed ahead to Gatwick and landed there. We borrowed another helicopter from Air Hanson, which was based at Gatwick, to complete the journey. I always looked forward to seeing Anne and I got on very well with Tom, twenty years her senior, whom she married in 1962. He was a successful racehorse owner and breeder with a stud at Heads Farm at Chaddleworth near Newbury. He bred many useful horses including *Final Chord* which completed a hat-trick of wins in 1974 when landing the Britannia Stakes at Royal Ascot under Joe Mercer. Tom would sometimes let me name one of his foals and I would try to come up with something suitable derived from the names of its sire and dam. For example, a foal which was by *High Hat* out of *Past Folly* I named *Cardinal Error*; another, by *Celtic Ash* out of *Mara River* I named *Burn*. After Tom retired in the 1990s, his son and my nephew, Charles took on the running of Heads Farm.

On 4 April 1970, still heavily relying on crutches, I passed my '1179', completing the necessary air hours to enable me to fly solo. The plan with XO was to hire it out with a pilot, Ron Salt, during the week while I was working and then to use it myself at weekends. The day after I qualified, John Dickin had arranged with me to take XO to Old Sarum to give one of his clients a lesson. This seemed too good an opportunity to miss and Susie I went with him. Within forty minutes of leaving Battersea at lunchtime, I landed outside the dining room window at Clarendon – quite a homecoming. A couple of weekends later, Susie was brave enough to be my passenger as I flew solo for the first time. We flew from Biggin Hill, where Ron had left XO, to Buxted Park Hotel in East Sussex where I was to receive some treatment for my leg. It wasn't the easy flight I might have had hoped for as a relative novice, taking the controls for the first time without an experienced pilot by my side. My log book records that we, 'Left Biggin and encountered very bad weather, low cloud and only just reached Buxted by hedge hopping.' I put my training to good use and landed safely. We stayed at Buxted until Monday but took the Sunday afternoon out to 'drop in' on friends and on my sister Clare and her husband Peter at their home in Dummer, Hampshire. On the way back we decided to pay Anne and Tom a quick visit at Heads Farm before going on to see Ian and Mary Cameron. We returned to Heads Farm the following weekend and, on the way, made a special delivery. The Todhunters were friends of the family who lived quite close to Heads Farm and my sister, Clare, had asked me to drop off a present for them. I didn't land at their farm but hovered as the box containing the gift was lowered to the ground. Inside the box was a tortoise.

Weekends became great fun. Journeys by helicopter took a fraction of the time they would have by road and I was able to visit friends in different parts of the country with ease – often paying more than one visit on any one day. Of course, having a helicopter arrive on one's front lawn was something of a novelty and many of my friends wanted to go up with me. It soon became quite common for me to pick them up from their homes and take them on somewhere for drinks or dinner. Understandably, the children of my friends would also want a ride and I was always happy to oblige whenever I could, though I always insisted on receiving written permission from their parents first.

Perhaps my most famous passenger was the Formula 1 champion, Jackie Stewart. On the last Saturday of April 1970, I flew Susie, Alexander McEwen and his wife Cecilia and our friend, Patricia Rawlings, to an international race day at Silverstone. Before going to the track we dropped in for lunch at Easton Neston, the home near Towcester of the flamboyant motor racing enthusiast Lord Hesketh who later formed his own Formula 1 team with the equally flamboyant James Hunt as his lead driver. Jackie Stewart was lunching there too. He was the reigning Formula 1 champion and undoubtedly the star turn of the event (in those days Formula 1 drivers would compete in all sorts of other races). Halfway through lunch Jackie excused himself as he had to make his way to the track and get ready for the day's racing. As he prepared to leave, I offered him a lift to the track. He accepted and in no time at all I delivered him to the pit lane, avoiding the long queues of traffic which had built up around the track. Patrick Lindsay of Christie's also came with us. Having dropped off my celebrity passenger I returned to Easton Neston to collect Susie, the McEwens and Patricia.

In early May, I visited my father and his new wife, Jocelyn, at the home they were setting up together near Orford in Suffolk. Susie and Caroline came as well and we stayed the Saturday night, returning to Gatwick on Sunday in poor visibility. The following weekend I landed XO within the walls of Warwick Castle where Susie and I enjoyed a lovely evening with David Brooke and his other guests, among them my cousin Sarah Henderson. The next day Sarah came with us to visit the Throckmortons at Coughton Court, the house on the edge of the Forest of Arden where the Gunpowder Plot was hatched. A most enjoyable weekend was rounded off with a visit to the Naylor-Leylands at Church Farm, Cirencester, where we stayed the night.

The next day, we flew with Michael Naylor-Leyland to Sudeley for drinks with Mark Brocklehurst and his wife, Elizabeth. I flew Mark over Sudeley Castle so that he could take some photographs of it. We then went back to Church Farm for lunch before taking Jakes, Michael's wife, on an aerial tour of Wiltshire, flying over Longleat, Stourhead, Fonthill, Wilton and Stonehenge.

G-AXXO parked inside the walls of Warwick Castle.

Having a helicopter also made it possible to see friends on the Continent without having to endure a tiresome ferry crossing or a long drive. I first ventured into foreign air space on Whitsun weekend, 1970, when Susie and I visited my great friends Teddy and Tanis Phillips at their home, Domaine de Migron, near Biarritz. Both in their sixties, Tanis was the younger sister of Loel Guinness and Teddy, Tanis' third husband, had served with the Royal Navy Volunteer Reserve during the war, attaining the rank of lieutenant commander. We first made the short hop to Gatwick where we were required to pass through customs. This took us about half an hour before we took off again, taking the long sea route to France over the Isle of Wight and the Cotentin Peninsula. Normally, one would take the shortest route possible over water. However, as we were making for south-west France, a crossing over the Straits of Dover would have made the flight to Biarritz considerably longer. As soon as we entered French air space, it became apparent, through a deathly silence on my radio, that all of the country's air traffic controllers were on strike, a not uncommon occurrence which has thwarted the travel plans of many. I hadn't been informed of the strike when I filed my flight plan but, fortunately, it didn't impede our progress at all and after a short refuelling stop at Nantes we reached Biarritz airport in good time. We were greeted by Teddy who had been awaiting our arrival in the control tower, which was eerily quiet with the controllers on strike. I was unable to fly directly to Teddy's house at Migron because, under French aviation law, one is only permitted to land at an airport, and not on private land. In Britain, I could land XO wherever I wanted, providing the landholder had given permission. Nonetheless, we arrived at Migron just in time for dinner.

The next day I flew Teddy and another of his guests, Adriano Miglietta, around the area. Adriano was an energetic ninety-year-old and in all my time at the controls of a helicopter I don't think I ever had an older passenger. He had made money in oil and had at one time been in business with John Cowdray's grandfather. Also there, was Liza Shaw, Tanis' daughter by her second marriage to the American, Howard Dietz, a well-known publicist, lyricist and librettist. Having spent a couple of very pleasant days at Migron, we offered Liza a lift back to England. The flight was not particularly easy as slight headwinds made it difficult to take the most direct route from Nantes to Gatwick. We landed at Cherbourg but the staff there were very slow and this made us late. We eventually arrived at Gatwick at 2050 hrs in failing light. Flying a helicopter demands absolute concentration and over long distances becomes very draining mentally. The last thing I needed at Gatwick was an over-zealous immigration officer. I recorded in my flight book: 'The Gatwick passport and immigration were exceptionally tiresome and difficult over Susie's Australian passport and Liza's American one. I might have been trying to smuggle in a boatload of illegal immigrants for all the fuss they made.' After thirty-five minutes in the company of these charming gentlemen, we were permitted to proceed to Battersea, landing in near darkness. I was quite exhausted.

Flying around Britain was much less stressful than venturing overseas. I did not have to endure frustrating delays at immigration control or customs and I could land almost anywhere I liked – for example, on a deserted stretch of beach on the north Cornwall coast. Early in June 1970, I took a house for the weekend, Treleven Cottage, at Polzeath where the Camel Estuary meets the sea. Susie and I left Battersea just before ten on the Friday morning with 'every kind of luggage including a picnic basket and television set.' I dropped her off at Heads Farm while I went on to a business meeting in Devizes; at that time I was on the board of a company which manufactured agricultural machinery, Archie Kidd Ltd. I would quite often fly to business meetings and remember once landing in the car park of Huntley

& Palmers in Reading, something which caused quite a stir among the staff there. On this particular day, I was tied up at Archie Kidd until nearly 5 p.m. and then flew back to Chaddleworth to collect Susie. No more than an hour and ten minutes later, pushed along by an easterly wind, I landed in the garden of Treleven Cottage. It was a very hot weekend and the following morning, having refuelled at St Mawgan RAF base, we went to St Mawes for lunch at a hotel recommended by a friend. Earlier in the week, from my office in London, I had arranged a landing site for XO with a garage in the town. After lunch we flew along the coast looking for a good beach. Penhale Sands, between Perranporth and Newquay is two and a half miles long. There is no vehicular access to its northern reaches which are consequently very quiet. This is where I chose to land, putting XO down just on the high water mark. We had a vast expanse of beach to ourselves

On the beach at Penhale Sands.

for the afternoon; there was no one within four hundred yards of us and probably only half a dozen people within a mile. We returned to the same spot the following day, our last at Polzeath, taking a huge picnic with Pimms and an ice bucket. On the way back to London, I refuelled at Exeter and, as we were so close, I flew over the site of my old school at Shobrooke Park which hadn't been rebuilt after the fire. Just the terrace remained standing but I could clearly make out the footprint of the old building. It felt strange coming back after so many years, a quarter of a century, and memories of that most dramatic night came flooding back. We flew on to stay with Anne and Tom for the night before heading back to Battersea on Tuesday morning. It was another boiling hot day and an early morning heat haze over London reduced visibility to almost nil. I reached Battersea by following the Thames at an altitude of about a hundred feet and had to ask for guidance from London Radar in the Control Zone.

Next, it was to the Continent again and a very eventful trip to Wiler, a small village in the Swiss Alps, where David Blackwell, a great friend of mine from the City, had a lodge. Along with Susie and David, my pilot, Ron Salt and another friend, Caroline Birkbeck also came. Ron had been out with XO on a charter flight that day and, consequently, we didn't get away from Battersea until 1845 hrs. The weather was atrocious and deteriorating all the time with heavy thunderstorms. I had intended to make for the airport at Avallon, a small town west of Dijon but it soon became apparent that we wouldn't make it in daylight. We crossed the Channel in thick cloud and the weather deteriorated still further as we reached the French coast. The plan now was to land at Le Touquet and to stay at David's flat there. However, as visibility decreased to about thirty metres, even this seemed unlikely and fearful of crashing into tall trees, I seized an opportunity to put XO down in a field in Montreuil, eventually positioning it in a farmyard. I reported the incident to the airport at Le Touquet and, having done all I could, we took a taxi to David's.

The following morning we drove back to Le Touquet airport from where, as I recorded at the time, 'a tremendous French drama ensued.' We were escorted back to Montreuil by three cars carrying controllers, customs officials, le commandant and police; there were more police waiting for us at the farm. It

Gendarmes, controllers and customs officials at a loss what to do after my 'illegal' landing in Montreuil. My friend, David Blackwell, is far right.

seemed no one was familiar with the procedures for dealing with my illegal landing and there was much scratching of heads and Gallic shrugging of shoulders. David was with me and we spent an hour and a half in the kitchen of the farmhouse explaining the necessity of our actions to the assembled throng of French officialdom which finally comprised thirteen people. Eventually, short of any other solution to the problem, the bemused authorities gave us permission to take off and we flew the short hop to Le Touquet to collect Susie and Caroline. From there we made for Geneva, via the military airport at Dijon, where, as I remember, the omelettes were quite good. On the way into Geneva, we were afforded an excellent view of the *Jet d'Eau*, the city's famous water fountain. After a frustrating delay at customs at Geneva airport, we finally left for the Lötschental Valley and Wiler, flying over Lake Geneva and then up the Rhine Valley. The final few miles of the journey were something of a struggle. David's apartment block was at six thousand feet and, at that altitude where the air is thin, helicopters lose some of their lift – particularly if, like mine, they are carrying five adults and plenty of luggage. We made it, but with very little power to spare.

Despite concerns about XO's performance at altitude, an opportunity to fly over the Alps was simply too good to resist. The following day, and lighter without our luggage, I flew high above the snowy caps of the Bernese Alps, taking in a spectacular view of the Bietschorn, a formidable pyramid of a mountain which, at nearly 13,000 feet dwarfs all those around it. It was among the most magnificent sights I ever saw during my years as a pilot. The exertions of flying at such heights must have taken their toll on XO. For when we came to leave Wiler the following

To the Skies

Flying over the Bietschorn in the Bernese Alps.

morning I found that it had a flat battery. Fortunately, one of David's neighbours plucked the battery from the local bus so that we could give XO a jump start. The flight home was no less eventful than the one out. I calculated that we were a little short of fuel for Geneva so decided to stop at Sion airport, just thirty miles or so from Wiler. Normally, a quiet airport, on this particular day, Sion was hosting an air rally and having refuelled we took off in 'a cloud of light aircraft.' Geneva airport was tiresome again and while waiting for clearance we took what I described at the time as 'an expensive and filthy lunch.' From there, I had intended to fly up the Loire Valley but deteriorating weather and poor visibility scuppered this plan. I made another stop to take on fuel at Orléans military airport, where, despite radioing ahead, our arrival caused a great deal of excitement. We were greeted by French soldiers waving machine guns at us. If this wasn't alarming enough, the ground staff there over-filled XO's tank resulting in the formation of a dangerous large puddle of aviation fuel under one of its landing skids. Eventually, we took off again and after a mercifully uneventful stop at Le Touquet we got back to Battersea at 1940 hrs. I was very tired after so much challenging flying.

Each flight, whether a short hop or a longer trip to the Continent required careful planning. I enjoyed poring over maps and charting the route I would take. Fuel was, of course, the most important factor to take in consideration. When flying in France, where I was only permitted to land at airports this presented few problems, but when I was flying around Britain and landing on the lawns of friends I had to factor in short hops to local airfields or airports to fill up with Avtur (Aviation Turbine Fuel). Providing I had done my homework, this rarely caused me any difficulties, though, on one occasion, it did prove troublesome. One weekend early in July 1970, Susie, Daška, Arabella and I had been visiting my father in Suffolk (Caroline was suffering with measles and had been unable to come with us). My father and Jocelyn were in the middle of a major renovation of their new house and we stayed at a pub in Orford. The following morning, Daška and I left early to try to find somewhere to refuel. There is no shortage of airfields in Suffolk, and I had planned to drop in on one of the American Air Force bases. One thing I had failed to consider was the date – it was 5 July, the day following Independence Day. It seemed the entire Suffolk-based US Air Force was nursing an almighty hangover and was unable, or unwilling, to oblige my requests to land. Thankfully, my own countrymen at RAF Wattisham were altogether more accommodating and were rewarded for their efforts by a guided tour of XO enthusiastically conducted by Daška. With a full tank, we flew back Orford to collect my father, Jocelyn and Susie and we then went to Capel to visit my cousin, Johnny Cobbold, the colourful chairman of Ipswich Town Football Club.

Le Touquet had been a favourite weekend destination since that glorious summer spent at Acrise. Now that I had a helicopter, it became much easier to reach. At the end of July 1970, I flew Susie, Daška and Arabella (poor Caroline was still recovering from measles) over the Channel to stay with David Blackwell. Having cleared customs at Gatwick, we took off, weighed down with supplies for the weekend. Low cloud made visibility poor on the French side of the Channel and I had to fly along the beach to Le Touquet at low altitude. The weather improved over the weekend and we flew around locally and up and down the coast, often at low altitude, so low, in fact, that XO's

Flying low along the beaches of northern France – so low that I cut through the string of a child's balloon with my rotors.

rotors cut through the string of a balloon which was being held by a rather bemused young girl standing on a beach.

Susie and I returned to Le Touquet in June of the following year, 1971, and used it as a stepping stone from which to explore more of France. Over the course of the weekend, we flew to Rheims and from there to DijonVal-Suzon airport in the Burgundy region. The following morning, we flew the short distance from Dijon Val-Suzon, a civil airport, to Dijon military airport, to refuel. Here, we were delayed for more than two hours by the arrival by air, just fifteen minutes later, of the French prime minister and ten other ministers. The delay was frustrating as we were intending to fly all the way back to Battersea that day. We eventually got away at 1530 hrs and made it back to London at 2005 hrs, refuelling at Tours. *En route*, we just had time to take a delightful lunch at the Auberge St Jacques in Orléans and then to fly all down the Loire Valley, taking in spectacular views of its châteaux, including Chambord, Chenonceau and Azay le Rideau.

Château de Chenonceau.

During the first summer I had XO, scarcely a weekend would pass without a trip somewhere to see friends and family or to attend other social events. Those on the ground were not always pleased to see me coming in to land. One weekend I flew Susie, Anne and Tom to Newbury Racecourse where one of Anne's horses was running. These days, helicopters are a common sight on racecourses as they bring in influential owners and top jockeys and the centre of many courses is given over to them for landing. Back then, this was not the case and at Newbury there was no designated landing zone; I simply had to find a space big enough for a helicopter in the public areas surrounding the track. XO, no doubt, caught the eye of parties of racegoers as I came in to land, but for one particular party, this fascination soon turned into horror as the downdraught from XO's rotors disintegrated their picnic sending sandwiches and paper plates flying in all directions. Ladies who had taken great care over their appearance for the day emerged from the carnage I had caused looking positively dishevelled.

Of course, having a helicopter made an enormous difference to me once the grouse shooting season opened. Towards the end of August I made my way up to Scotland, visiting friends on the way, to shoot with Lord Linlithgow on his estate in South Lanarkshire, Leadhills. I left my helicopter at Lamington in a field near my friends and cousins, the Leslie-Melvilles, and drove the short distance to Leadhills with Charlie Hambro. Among Lord Linlithgow's other guests was my uncle, Cosmo Crawley, the father of my dear cousin, Sarah. I stayed at Leadhills for four days. It was very hot, in fact too hot to shoot grouse successfully as a lot wouldn't get up and certainly wouldn't fly twice. Despite this, I shot well from a good draw. Later in the week, I brought my helicopter up to Leadhills so that I could make a quick getaway after our final drive. My destination was Wentworth Woodhouse in South Yorkshire to see Tom and Joyce Fitzwilliam, an arduous three and a half hour drive by car but a mere hour and a quarter by air. I left Leadhills at 1720 hrs and arrived in good time to change for dinner.

The arrangement I had with Ron Salt broadly allowed him to use XO during the week for chartered work, while I flew at weekends. This inevitably caused us both a few difficulties. Ron received many enquiries for weekend work, enquiries he quite often had to turn down, while I, particularly during the shooting season, would have liked to have had use of the machine on weekdays. During the first working week of September 1970, I had no alternative but to drive to Dunecht for my annual stay with John Cowdray because Ron was using XO. I have to say that, in general, our arrangement had a more adverse effect on Ron's activities than they did on mine: I flew purely for pleasure and convenience; for Ron flying was his livelihood. Between us, scheduling flying time required a great deal of planning and one of us would quite often take over from the other without even turning the engine off. For example, one weekday in November 1970, I needed XO to fly to Milton in Northamptonshire to shoot with Tom Fitzwilliam. I had hitched a lift with Charlie Hambro and John Dickin, from the heliport at St Katherine's Dock to Battersea where Ron was waiting with XO's rotors already turning. Ron had been flying all day and I took off at 1645 hours, allowing just enough time to reach Milton in daylight. Though Ron and I managed our arrangements as best we could, it became increasingly clear that neither one of us was getting as much from XO as we would have liked. The solution to this problem seemed simple: later, I bought a second helicopter which I leased, during the week, to a second pilot. As I only needed one helicopter at any given time, this gave the two pilots an even chance of being able to accept weekend charter work and increased my chances of being able to use one machine during the week if I needed to. By the summer of 1972, I had three helicopters and I set up a company, Heli Air Ltd., to manage their activities. One, call sign G-AWRV (RV), went out on a long-term lease to Plessey in September 1972; it was even painted in Plessey's corporate colours.

Before I assembled this small fleet, Charlie Hambro would often help me out, ferrying me around in his own helicopter so that I could rendezvous with Ron. Charlie was a great friend as well as being my cousin and we shared a love of both shooting and flying helicopters. I spent many happy days on his estate in Gloucestershire, Dumbleton. I noted in my game book that the year 1970 was perhaps the best year for game at Dumbleton since the war and, on 23 November, our party which also included Mark Brocklehurst, shot nearly seven hundred pheasants. The weather forecast for that day had been bad, but luckily the rain held off and the wind abated. The previous night I had lain awake, worried about XO's well-being as the wind howled outside; I had parked it in an exposed field in Dixton and was fully expecting to find it blown over when I returned to it in the morning. Fortunately, it survived the battering. I would often take my daughters to Dumbleton; Charlie also had three children and the six together always got on famously.

Invariably, wherever I was flying to, I would return to one of the London airports or heliports; Heathrow, Gatwick, Battersea or St Katherine's. Over time, my call sign became familiar to those whose job it was to control the traffic in the skies above London. Consequently, I received a very generous invitation, which was not often extended, to pay a visit to the control tower at Heathrow. On Sunday 21 February (Sundays were quieter then than they are now) Susie and I landed at Heathrow where we were met at the Pan Am hanger and driven over to the control tower. We spent an hour and a half with the controllers who explained and demonstrated just how they directed traffic in the world's busiest airspace. It was all tremendously interesting and just a little frightening to consider that just one small technical or operational lapse in this nerve centre could lead to an awful disaster.

Flying and shooting were my two great passions. Never was the connection between these activities closer than one August weekend in 1971. On the Friday, I received the following telegram;

> Message from Mr [Johnny] Johnstone of Westland Heliport regarding pigeon shoot on Saturday. It is OK with the police – morning is best because it will be low tide at 09:29 so any time before ten and for the next three or four hours.

At that time, Westland, the helicopter manufacturer owned and operated the heliport at Battersea. The invitation from Johnny Johnstone was to bring my gun to Battersea for some sport on the banks of the Thames. Pigeons could be quite a nuisance to aircraft in London and their increasing numbers around Battersea were causing Johnny concerns over safety; a bird strike on an outgoing or incoming helicopter might have catastrophic consequences. Knowing I was a keen shot, Johnny thought I was the ideal person to help rid the heliport of this threat. I gleefully accepted his invitation and arrived at Battersea with my gun in the boot of my car at low tide on Saturday morning. It was great fun. I was able to walk up and down the river's edge for several hundred yards in each direction and the weather was clear and bright. I managed to shoot forty-five pigeons. In so doing however, I made rather a lot of noise, a noise that the residents of that part of London were not particularly used to early on a Saturday morning. Some interest was shown in my activities but only one complaint was made. When the police arrived to follow up this complaint, they approached me and asked what I was doing. I simply replied, 'pest control officer' which seemed to satisfy them and they left me to get on with the job. The entry in my game book for the following morning reads; 'Continued my unselfish role as the public pest officer, giving up a Sunday morning to do so.' Having shot a good number of pigeons, I flew off to have lunch with some friends. Upon my return to Battersea that evening, I noticed that there were still quite a few birds around. I had my gun in the back of XO and, having landed, I shot four more before the rotors had stopped turning. My tally for the weekend was 98 pigeons and this figure would have been higher had I not run out of cartridges. I reprised my role as pest controller at Battersea on a number of subsequent occasions. I remember one particularly successful hour at the end of October,

'Pest Control Officer' at Battersea Heliport.

just a few days after Susie had given birth to our first child together, my fourth daughter, Susannah. I picked Susie up from hospital and decided to take her, together with Arabella who must have been on holiday from school, to Battersea for some fresh air.

I hit 56 pigeons in an hour, much to the amusement of Arabella, though I'm not sure what my new-born daughter made of the whole thing. In all, in my role as an inner city pest controller I killed more than two hundred pigeons.

I had first shot pigeons as a young boy at Clarendon, building a hide out of straw bales. I have happy and vivid memories of those times and I remember one particular instance when a sparrow hawk swooped at lightning speed and severed the head of a pigeon I had shot as it was plummeting towards the ground. In adult life, in addition to my activities on the banks of the Thames, I would occasionally shoot pigeons with a professional who was engaged by farmers to control the rural population of these pests who threatened their crops. His name was Major Archie Coats (ex Scots Guards) and he lived in Dummer, a village I visited often to see both my father (before he moved to Suffolk) and my sister, Clare. Archie travelled from farm to farm across Hampshire and the Home Counties shooting more or less seven days a week. He was a well-loved character and a master of his craft, described recently as 'the doyen of pigeon shooting.' His maxim, renowned in shooting circles, was, 'Think like a pigeon.' At the time I started to shoot with him, Archie held the unofficial record for pigeons killed in a single day. One January day in 1962, he bagged no fewer than 550 and this figure would have been even higher had he not run out of shells twice. Archie would sometimes invite me to help him out and we shot together quite regularly from the late sixties and through the seventies. It was great fun: Archie knew every trick in the book and I learned a great deal from him. For example, when we were shooting from the same hide he introduced me to a clever strategy for beguiling the pigeons into a false sense of security. Archie was an expert at deploying decoys, dead birds held upright on short sticks which he would position carefully in a field of crops. The pigeons, seeing the decoys would assume that all was safe in the field and come in to land and feed. At this point Archie and I would hold our fire and wait for a second wave of birds to come in. When they did, we would shoot at these latecomers and still have enough time to kill two birds from the advance party as they flew away. Employing this method often enabled us to get four birds at a time. On other occasions, we would work from separate hides or positions at either end of a field in order to increase our chances of success. Sometimes, my father, who knew Archie well, would join us and we would form a triangle over a considerable area which left the pigeons nowhere to escape to. My brother-in-law Peter Wilmot-Sitwell also came with us on one occasion. Archie was quite a character, seldom seen without a pipe in his mouth and great fun to be with. What he didn't know about pigeon shooting wasn't worth knowing and, in 1984, he was the subject of an entire episode of *Jack's Game*, a television programme devoted to fieldsports hosted by the footballer, Jack Charlton.

Just a few days after my first pigeon shoot at Battersea in early August, XO very nearly crashed in the heart of London during evening rush hour. The story was picked up by the *Evening Standard* which reported it in the following terms: 'A helicopter made a forced landing into the River Thames last night. Only quick thinking by the pilot stopped it hitting a bridge crowded with home going Londoners.' The 'quick-thinking pilot' was not me but Major Mike Somerton-Rayner. This incident happened after I had bought a second machine and had entered into an arrangement with Mike which was similar to the one I had with Ron Salt. Mike had been flying three racegoers back to London from Salisbury when a compressor in XO's engine blew up three hundred feet above Wandsworth Bridge. The engine failed immediately and only Mike's quick thinking averted disaster. When the *Standard* interviewed him, he explained that, 'When the engine stopped I immediately went into auto-rotation – putting the blades into a certain angle so that you can glide instead of stopping.' Using this technique, one that all helicopter pilots must practise, he managed to land the machine on its floats on the river, avoiding the bridge and river traffic. A rubber dinghy took Mike and his passengers to shore and I arrived not long afterwards to find XO bobbing up and down on the river unmanned. It was soon towed ashore by the river police and went off to be repaired.

G-AXXO safely bobbing on the Thames thanks to the quick thinking of pilot, Mike Somerton-Rayner.

XO was out of service for about a month, while my other machine (I hadn't acquired the third at this time) was in great demand from Ron and Mike. The accident had happened on 11 August, the eve of the grouse shooting season and for a short while I returned to dashing around the country by car in order to shoot. I went first to Wentworth Woodhouse where I stayed for three days' enjoyable shooting and then drove up to Leadhills for four more. I spent the last of eight consecutive days' shooting at Eyemouth, a fishing village in the Borders. With a few friends, among them Alexander McEwen, I took a small boat out from the harbour and we shot quite a few pigeon together with various other birds, mostly cormorants. It was all tremendous fun and it was about 9 p.m. by the time we returned.

As well as Susie, the children and my friends, there was another 'frequent flyer' in XO. Zippo, like dear old Dan, a whippet, would often join us on our weekend travels and adventures, though of course, in a time before pet passports and microchips, we could never take him across to France and the Continent. I have to say that, fine companion though he was, Zippo was not always the easiest passenger. One day, he had been such a nuisance as we flew to lunch with friends in Dorking and then on to Henley that I recorded in my flying book, 'Zippo has become rather anti-flying.' Nonetheless, he continued to come with us whenever possible and he was very much part of a very happy family Christmas in 1971 spent with Anne and Tom at Heads Farm. First, I flew Susie, Susannah, Susannah's nanny and Zippo to Marlow where we spent Christmas Eve with my mother. After church on Christmas Day, we all squeezed into XO and went on to Chaddleworth. Christmas lunch was great fun and the whole family were there except for Daška, Caroline and Arabella who were spending Christmas with Marina. Marrying Susie had not affected my friendship with Marina and I continued to spend as much time with the three girls as I could. We have always had great fun together and, of course, at this time they had an adorable baby half-sister to dote on.

As another New Year dawned, my life continued in much the same vein. I was very happy and settled in my position as partner at Panmure Gordon and surrounded by good friends there and elsewhere in the City. I continued to devote my free time to family, shooting and flying – often combining all three together. The four or so years during which I flew helicopters were some of the most memorable of my life and browsing through the records I kept of my aerial adventures brings back many happy memories. I bought a third machine, like the others also a Bell 206A JetRanger, in the summer of 1972. It was a 1967 model which had been owned by Air Hanson with the call-sign G-AVZH. Its registration document records that it was acquired by my company, Heli Air Ltd. on 9 June 1972. Just three months later, it was to be in ZH that I would have my second air accident.

On 3 October 1972, I flew from London to Wiltshire to go to a country auction in a village called Coates near Cirencester. Michael Naylor-Leyland lived nearby and I stayed with him that night. Before leaving Michael the following morning, I telephoned Swindon for a weather report and was told that conditions were clear with only a light wind. As was often the case, my intention was to fill up ZH locally before heading back to London. The nearest airfield was an RAF base at South Cerney just a few miles south-west of Cirencester and a short hop from

Michael's. It was a fine morning and unusually warm for early October: on one side of the airport I remember seeing a man on the ground walking around with his shirt off at 8 o'clock in the morning. As I continued my descent at the other side of the airport however, I hit a thick bank of fog lying very close to the ground. This was unusual as fog tends to form around rivers, in valleys or on hills, not on level ground such as an airfield. Two options were available to me: either I could ascend and attempt to fly over the fog or I could descend very slowly and try to land. I was flying very slowly, at perhaps only twenty knots and at a very low altitude, no more than thirty feet and I decided to land, hoping that if I inched my way down the fog would clear six feet or so from the ground. It didn't and I hit the ground before I could even see it. The right leg of ZH hit first and the strut broke. This caused the machine to fall forward and the rotor hit the ground next. It disintegrated on impact and shrapnel from it was sent flying in all directions at great speed. If any part of it had come in my direction it would have certainly killed me. I had crashed on the edge of the airfield and, because the fog was so thick, nobody in the hangers or the control buildings saw what happened. Neither did they hear it as the impact was relatively soft and there was no loud bang or explosion. The fog was so thick that I had very little idea where I was and I made my way gingerly to the nearest road. Later, I was unable to find my way back to the wreck of ZH. When I reached the road, I made way along it for a short distance and, through the gloom, I spied a cottage where a family were building their garage, apparently dressed in their pyjamas. It must have been quite a shock for them a few minutes earlier when a large section of my rotor whizzed past them and imbedded itself in the structure. The machine was a write-off but I emerged completely unscathed. The Civil Aviation Authority records all air accidents, however minor, and I recently had a look at its report of mine. The records for both bear the words, 'Fatalities 0 / Occupants 1', rather like a football result: fortunately both results went in my favour.

    I continued to fly after the accident, though with ZH written off and RV out to Plessey, I was back down to one machine, my beloved XO. I continued to fly for a further two years or so and only gave it up following the stock market crash of 1974, which was triggered by the OPEC oil crisis during which the price of a barrel soared from $3 to $12. At this time, it became rather unseemly and a little ostentatious to be seen turning up to meetings in a helicopter when so many people were suffering great hardship during a deep recession. For this reason, charter work also began to dry up. Under these circumstances I took the difficult decision to sell my two remaining machines and though I did this with some regret, it was certainly the right thing to do. My days as a pilot, of either aeroplanes or helicopters, had come to an end.

5. The Middle Years

I turned 40 in 1974, and Susie and I celebrated the occasion on safari in Kenya. This wasn't a planned trip at all. A great friend of mine, Stas (Stanislaw) Radziwill, had arranged the trip and had intended to go with another mutual friend, Harry Ashcombe. At the last moment Harry couldn't go and so Stas invited us to join him instead. We went for three weeks and had a marvellous time. Nowadays, hunting in Africa is largely frowned upon and it is illegal to hunt many of that continent's endangered species. Back in 1974, however, there were fewer restrictions and the Masai Mara was a popular destination for those who, like me, were keen shots and who wanted to test their aim and nerve in a genuinely wild environment. During the course of our stay, we killed a wide variety of animals, including buffalo, wildebeest, zebra, impala, topi, a leopard and wart hogs and we saw many more.

I killed three buffalo in all and these were perhaps the most prized quarry of the trip; buffalo are extremely dangerous adversaries, very difficult to kill and possessed of a particularly acute sense of revenge. The first we came across was the most tenacious beast I think I have ever encountered. One day early in the trip, we left our camp at dawn and before long we spotted a herd of buffalo some distance away across a gorge. We moved in stealthily and when we were within range I took aim and fired at one of the herd with a .458 Winchester, a very powerful rifle designed for big game. My quarry moved slightly just as I fired and consequently the bullet passed straight through its shoulder;

The Middle Years

With Susie and our guides over our first buffalo in Kenya.

it was no more than two inches away from killing it outright. We lost sight of the wounded beast but followed its blood trail into the forest, moving slowly and with great care. We soon found it again and it appeared to be waiting for us with a vengeful look in its eyes. Before it had chance to charge us, Susie and I fired at it at the same time, both shots hitting. Even this failed to finish it off and, after tracking it through the forest for a further half an hour, we both fired again, this time missing. The buffalo had, by this time, lost an awful lot of blood and was very weak. Taking great care, I was able to get up very close to it and finished it off with a shot through the neck. Stalking it had been very exciting and had been fraught with danger. I was staggered at how tough the animal was; any of the previous three shots which had hit should have been sufficient to kill it.

My birthday itself was a lovely day, though I very nearly didn't make 40. The day before, we had been stalking buffalo again, this time unsuccessfully. On the way back to our camp we came across some elephants in the forest which were very close. Too close. They spotted us. There are few things more frightening than a herd of rampaging elephants and this particular herd charged us twice. In flight, my hat blew off. I didn't bother to attempt to retrieve it. The following day, having narrowly survived into my forties, we stalked and killed another buffalo, butchering it afterwards so that we could take its meat back for dinner. We hoisted its legs up a tree to be used as bait for the animal we were hoping to find more than any other, a leopard. We used a warthog I shot in a similar fashion and though this made a total of twelve leopard baits hung up in an area where we were told leopards roamed, we were yet to see one of these imperious large cats. We took a late lunch, building a fire and cooking buffalo liver, which was a little tough for my liking. Later, we returned to camp where preparations were underway to throw a lavish birthday party for me. Huge fires were lit, a lamb was barbecued, champagne flowed freely and I even had a birthday cake. All in all, it was a marvellous day.

I was feeling a little worse for wear the following day, something I attributed at the time to a 'bad bacon sandwich' rather than to too much champagne the previous evening. We spent the day looking for elephant with our Masai guide, Kilamoy, whom Susie took something of a shine towards. We didn't find any, but when we returned to camp at 3 p.m., we learned that an impala which had been hung up as leopard bait

The Middle Years

had been eaten. We immediately set out on its trail, reaching a blind (hide) at about 5. Nothing happened there, except for two things: first, a rhino came to within a few paces of the blind and started nibbling at it; second, I was sick. We left the blind just after 7, a little disappointed. Then, in fading light, we saw a leopard just a short distance away facing us. I raised my rifle and shot it just under the chin. Then, it disappeared. One of our party fired off another two shots which missed. As we edged forward it became clear that my shot had killed the leopard which was half down a hole. This caused great excitement and we returned to camp in high spirits though I was still a little green around the gills.

With a leopard.

The following day we went looking for elephants again. I had a licence to shoot them but I had made my mind up that I would only take the opportunity if I came across one that was old and sick. I didn't encounter one in this condition but, that day, we did get rather too closer for comfort to a large herd for the second time. While walking in an area where we had been told there were elephants, we suddenly found ourselves in amongst a herd of twenty or so without even knowing it. They were lying down in tall grass and we could smell them. They spotted us and, as one, arose and charged in all directions, including ours. The sound was thunderous and the ground shook as they charged. I'm not sure I have ever run so fast in my entire life.

The last few days on safari were a little disappointing but I enjoyed our holiday immensely. Kenya is breathtakingly beautiful and hunting in the Masai certainly got one's blood pumping. Of course, during this period, my life wasn't all about flying and shooting. I was settled as a partner at Panmure Gordon and was enjoying my work enormously among many great friends. During the early 1970s, we acted successfully for Grand Metropolitan, Allied Breweries and Bass during the so-called 'brewery battles', acrimonious corporate contests which completely changed the shape of Britain's brewing industry. The early 1970s were a very volatile period in Britain's history both, politically and economically; the miners' strike and the three day week brought uncertainty to the markets and this was followed by the OPEC oil crisis of 1973 which led to the price of a barrel soaring from $3 to $12 within the space of just six months. It was an exciting time in the City and one had to be on one's toes. At Panmure Gordon, though we all worked extremely hard, there were still opportunities to have some fun in the office. Ever slightly mischievous, I was often the architect of office pranks and one individual in particular became the target of my practical jokes.

Brian (pronounced Bree-an) MacDermot was four years older than me and had joined Panmure as a partner shortly before I arrived from Williams de Broë. He had a passionate interest in the peoples and culture of east and central African having served there with the Irish Guards and, during the time I worked with him, he would spend almost all of his spare time travelling to Ethiopia and Sudan where he would 'go native.' In 1972, he spent some time living among the Nuer pastoralists of the Nile Valley and concluded, with an air of characteristic pomposity, that 'it was possible to become almost totally accepted by a primitive people.' Whenever he returned from his expeditions he would go on about them in the office *ad nauseam.* He was also obsessed with the royal family and a practising Catholic. A chance encounter with an old flame, one day, gave me a spark of inspiration to play a joke on MacDermot: one which would appeal to all of his interests and 'virtues' and one which all in the office except him were in on.

The lady in question was named Jo, an ex-girlfriend whom I hadn't seen for a very long time until I happened to bump into her in the late autumn of 1974. It was after she had told me that she was working at Lambeth Palace as secretary to the Archbishop of Canterbury that my scheme began to take shape. I certainly wouldn't have been able to take it further without her willingness to help and her complete discretion. On 11 December, MacDermot received the following letter from Lambeth Palace. It was signed on behalf of the Domestic Chaplain there but, of course, had been written by me and typed up by Jo on Lambeth Palace letterhead.

Dear Mr MacDermot,

His Grace the Archbishop of Canterbury has asked me to write to you to request a special favour.

Your work on behalf of the Royal Anthropological Society has come to his Grace's attention, equally your very interesting travels, writings and films of Central Africa. This is a subject of great personal interest to the Archbishop.

We have here an annual Christmas party for underprivileged children of all denominations held at Lambeth Palace on Monday, 6th January 1975. The Archbishop is hoping to be honoured by the attendance this year of a member of the Royal Family.
Apart from tea and games, His Grace would like to show something of educational interest particularly concerning people from other lands, especially as the children themselves will come from many different parts of the world

It is in this connection that the Archbishop is hoping you will help us for this very worthwhile cause by giving a short talk accompanied by films for, say, 35 to 40 minutes.

The Archbishop realises that this is too short for you to cover fully any one subject, but we are wondering whether we shall be able to hold all the children's attention for longer than this.

In his first year as Primate, the Archbishop particularly hopes this party will be a success and that you would be kind enough to assist us. He realises what an imposition this will be on a busy man such as yourself.

Yours sincerely, etc.

The bait had been laid. African scholar, royalist and man of faith – I had worded the letter to appeal to all that made MacDermot tick. It worked, and what was more, he brought the letter into the office, gathered forty or so of his colleagues around him and read it out. I had confided my joke to most, if not all, of those gathered and we all found it difficult to keep a straight face as MacDermot imparted the 'Archbishop's' request for his help and announced his impending appointment with royalty. His response to this first letter was immediate. Jo, whose job involved opening all the post received at Lambeth Palace, intercepted the letter before it could reach the 'real' Domestic Chaplain and then sent it on to me. MacDermot had taken the bait, hook, line and sinker. He unctuously expressed his willingness to be of assistance and was keen to emphasise that his anthropological work had already received royal approval from the late Prince William of Gloucester, who assisted him in the making of his film, *The Tribes of Lake Rudolf*. MacDermot proposed showing this film but expressed doubts concerning its suitability for the Archbishop's guests. He wrote,

> I would certainly like to do what I can to help and I only hope that the material I would show will be appropriate. I should however warn you that although there is nothing which could to any degree be termed as pornographic in my film, naked tribesmen do appear on the screen from time to time.

This particular paragraph brought much hilarity to my colleagues in the office and I set about composing a suitable reply, delaying the next letter for some days for the sake of authenticity. Again writing as the Domestic Chaplain, I informed MacDermot that his letter had caused Lambeth Palace 'an embarrassing dilemma' which had been 'a matter of great deliberation between the Archbishop and my colleagues.' On balance, 'the Archbishop' had decided that the material MacDermot had proposed to show 'would not be completely suitable for his particular audience.' The 'Domestic Chaplain' explained why.

> For ourselves, although leading cloistered lives, we do consider we have a broad minded attitude to life. The embarrassment the Archbishop feels really concerns the lady attendants accompanying the children, some of who are Sisters of other Religious Orders and of course Her Royal Highness herself.

To keep the joke going, the letter concluded with effusive

The Middle Years

thanks, expressed the hope that a more suitable occasion might be found to show *The Tribes of Lake Rudolf* and promised further correspondence on the subject after Christmas (the letter was dated 20 December). MacDermot wasn't prepared to wait until after the holiday. He wrote to the Archbishop two days before Christmas absolving him of any embarrassment and offering his assistance in any future endeavours to support such a worthy cause. He also pledged assistance from both the Royal Anthropological Institute, of which he was a council member and chairman of its Development Committee, and the support of the Royal Geographical Society of which he was also a council member. He suggested that, at some future time, an evening of tribal music might go down well. I latched onto this point in my final letter as Domestic Chaplain in which I upped the stakes considerably. I informed him that his idea for an evening of tribal appealed greatly to 'me' personally, continuing,

> Although I cannot match your own knowledge of abroad, I well recall when I was first called to Holy Orders and was the incumbent of St Boniface's, Pitlochry, we had a similar and most successful evening. The strains of *O Come all ye Faithful!* sung by Highland voices accompanied only by bagpipes in candlelight remains one of the most moving experiences I have had whilst in His service.

I continued my flattery by asking MacDermot if he would become a sort of lay adviser to Lambeth Palace on business matters, an appointment which would, of course, need to remain in the strictest confidence. My closing words were as follows. 'I offer my best wishes for the New Year with kind personal regards. I feel our recent correspondence has been of a most fruitful and rewarding nature.' I didn't receive a reply to this last letter and as 1975 dawned, I couldn't quite work out why the correspondence had dried up. I felt certain MacDermot would have penned a reply to my last letter, but none ever reached me. Sometime later, I bumped into Jo again, and she said that she had neglected to inform me that she was only working at Lambeth Palace for three months. Of course, without her acting as my secretarial accomplice, any letters written by MacDermot which arrived at the Palace after she had left would have reached their intended recipient, the Domestic Chaplain himself. He, oblivious to the earlier flurry of correspondence going on in his name would have been a little confused to say the least. In all probability, the Domestic Chaplain must have written to MacDermot and asked him in very polite terms what on Earth he was on about. If this was the case, MacDermot certainly never told us that he had received a letter from a rather bemused senior clergyman. Though why would he, when such an admission would only make him appear foolish and gullible? That assumes, of course, that he realised that he had been set up. One thing I am sure of is that he never learned that I was behind the entire thing or that the whole office was in on the elaborate joke.

Poor MacDermot was very gullible and was the butt of every practical joke, not only at Panmure but also at Cazenove's where he was before. Indeed, long before he started in the City, someone played a practical joke on him while he was doing his National Service back in the fifties. While he was cleaning the windows of a Nissen hut during his basic training at Caterham, one of his fellow cadets (me) advised him that he would get a better shine if he set light to the cleaning fluid.

Not long after the 'Lambeth Palace' letters, I seized an opportunity to play another joke on MacDermot, one which had an immediate effect. In the office one day, I knew that he had a lunch appointment with a Mr Talbot Rice, a senior investment manager and one of Panmure's important clients. MacDermot had arranged the appointment some weeks earlier and had been going on about it interminably. We were all a bit fed up with this and so I decided that both MacDermot and his client should have a lunch date that neither would be likely to forget. It was one of those blustery days when showers alternated with sunny spells. As MacDermot was getting to ready to leave to meet Mr Talbot Rice, I said to him, 'Don't forget to take your umbrella. It looks like rain.' He took my advice and I sat back in my office and hoped for the best. To my delight, before long I could see raindrops on the office windows and though I didn't witness the scene, in true MacDermot style, the man himself related what had happened in great detail when he returned later. MacDermot was quite a demonstrative man. As he was walking side by side with Mr Talbot Rice, he felt the first drops of rain, and he raised his umbrella with theatrical flourish. Upon so doing, a shower of confetti and French letters rained down on both him and his client. One of the French letters lodged in the brim of Mr Talbot Rice's bowler hat and a man on the other side of the street laughed so much that he nearly suffered a heart attack. It was difficult to keep a straight face as, later, MacDermot told us about this bizarre incident and he never found out that it was me, with help from a colleague, David Mayhew, who had covertly and with great relish loaded the umbrella earlier that morning. Perhaps having had enough of being the victim of practical jokes, MacDermot left Panmure Gordon in 1976 to set up a gallery for Oriental and African art.

In between playing jokes, I did get some work done and during the seventies I moved into the institutional sales and corporate finance side of things at Panmure. I was still living at Seymour Walk with Susie and our two young daughters. From 1972 onwards, we also had a country retreat. In the spring of that year, Susie and I flew to Wiltshire to see a large house on the Bowood estate. I recorded at the time that the house, Buckhill, seemed 'very promising.' Not long afterwards I took a twenty-one year lease on the house, an arrangement which was to be reviewed every seven years. In the end, I kept it for over thirty years. It is a beautiful house with land, walled gardens and a tennis court which was a convenient landing pad for G-AXXO and I spent many happy times there. It was the perfect weekend retreat and we would often have friends to stay; on one occasion, I remember, it accommodated seventeen. On Friday evening, unless I was away shooting elsewhere, we would leave London for Buckhill House, weighed down with provisions, children, a cat, a dog and up to six goldfish which didn't corner very well. This became my weekend routine and I always looked forward to escaping to the country.

Buckhill House also had another distinct advantage. At about the same time as I took it, Marina was considering schools for Daška who would have been about eleven. Marina had narrowed the choice down to three schools, one in Yorkshire, one in Kent and a third, St Mary's Calne, just a short distance from

Country retreat. Buckhill House on the Bowood Estate which I took for over thirty years. G-AXXO is parked on the tennis court.

Bowood. At this time, Marina had no idea that I'd taken, or was about to take, the lease at Buckhill and I, of course, was very struck by the prospect that Daška would be at school just down the road from where I would be spending weekends and that, in all probability, her younger sisters would follow her there. To ensure that Marina made the 'right choice', I employed a little reverse psychology. I extolled the virtues of one of the other schools, the one in Yorkshire, knowing full well that Marina would want to have the final say and that she would probably not go along with my recommendation. Sure enough, the plan worked. I have only very recently confessed my tactics to Marina and I am pleased to say that she can see the funny side of it. I suggested the school in Yorkshire and Marina chose the school in Calne. However the decision came about, Marina's choice of St Mary's proved to be an excellent one. Daška thrived there, becoming Head Girl. Caroline and Arabella did indeed follow her there and also did very well. Being so close to Bowood the girls tended to spend more time with me at weekends than with Marina who was still living in London. They would often bring friends along with them and many of these still tell me how much they enjoyed their time with us there. Much later, my younger daughters, Sophie and Laura also did well at St Mary's, Sophie becoming the second Cobbold to be the school's Head Girl.

Susannah (born 1971) and Kate (born 1973), my daughters with Susie, didn't go to St Mary's. My marriage to Susie was never terribly straightforward for a number of reasons and we separated in about 1976 or 1977. It would be fair to say that this parting was neither as simple nor as cordial as when Marina and I had separated a decade or so earlier. Susie and the girls stayed in this country for a while but some time later Susie asked for my permission to take our daughters back to her native Australia. This came as quite a shock and I don't know what she might have done had I objected. After some deliberation and with a heavy heart I acquiesced and Susannah and Kate went off to Perth with their mother. They were schooled there but would come over to see me every holiday, though the arrangements I made to collect them from Heathrow did not always go smoothly. Neither was the long flight easy for the girls, particularly for Kate who suffered quite terribly from air sickness. The long summer holiday in Australia, of course, was during our winter and I would often take Susannah and Kate with me when I went shooting around the country. The rest of the time when they were on the other side of the world, I missed them very much and sometimes wonder if I ought to have stood my ground and not let them go. They both still live in Australia, having built successful lives for themselves, and they come over to visit me as often as they can. We are very close and they have always got on tremendously well with their other sisters and brother.

The other major upheaval that divorce with Susie brought concerned the house at Seymour Walk. The financial settlement reached between our lawyers required me to sell this magnificent house which I had restored some fifteen year earlier. It had been the perfect family home and though, at the time I bought it, it was considered to be in a rather unfashionable part of London, SW10 became, and remains, a very exclusive address. More importantly, it was a wonderful place to bring up a family and I have many happy memories of times spent with my children there. The settlement, however, meant that I could no longer afford to keep both Seymour Walk and Buckhill House. If I had been able to hang on to the former, today it would probably be worth something in the region of £12 million. I bought a smaller, though still very comfortable, house, in Vicarage Gardens just off Kensington Church Street. As things would turn out I wouldn't stay there long.

Shooting continued to play a very important part in my life. Though I no longer had a helicopter to get me around the country quickly, my shooting schedule remained as busy as it had ever been. I have always been the sort of man who wants to get from A to B as quickly as possible and now that I was again confined to travelling by road, I bought a series of very fast cars.

None was faster than a Ferrari 275 GTB, in grey and blue. Its acceleration from a 3.3 litre V12 engine was a match for my old Renault Dauphine, but once up to speed it handled significantly better. I got it up to 150 miles per hour on several occasions and, once, very nearly touched 160 on the Oxford Bypass, the A34. As well as the 275 GTB, I also had, at a later time, a Ferrari 400 which was a little more sedate, a Maserati Mistral which was quite unreliable and prone to overheating, an Aston Martin and the Bentley which had covered the journey from Cortina to Ostend in record time. Staying within the speed limit in any of these cars was a little difficult, yet I was never once stopped for speeding. The closest I came to being 'collared' was when I was driving to Wentworth Woodhouse to visit the Fitzwilliams. The weather was dreadful and as I sped north at an average speed over 100, I failed to spot a police car on the side of the road. It pulled out to pursue me and I noticed the flashing blue light through the rain pouring down my rear windscreen. I had two choices; either to slow down, pull over and take the lecture, fine and points on my licence, or to put my foot down and outrun the police. I chose the second of these options. In those days there were no speed cameras or devices to record registration plates and I suppose the only risk I faced was that as they trailed in my wake the police would radio for other vehicles to try to head me off further down the road. This didn't happen and they simply must have given up the chase.

If anything, I shot more regularly in the years after I had stopped flying than I had when I was hopping around the country by air. As well as my usual haunts, the Cowdray estates, Dumbleton, Wentworth Woodhouse, Nantclwyd, etc., I received

The Middle Years

invitations to shoot at many other places and I continued to meet some very interesting people and make new friends. Sadly, the older one gets the more often one has to deal with losing those closest to one and the sudden death in 1972 of one of my dearest friends, Mark Brocklehurst, came as a great shock and upset me deeply.

One of the advantages of having a house at Bowood was that I was very easily able to combine shooting with spending time with my family. Lord Shelburne would very kindly ask me to shoot pheasants on the estate with him during the winter months and if Susannah and Kate were over from Australia or Daška, Caroline or Arabella with me for the weekend from school, they would often come along too. Among others who regularly shot at Bowood were a couple of Tory Party grandees who became very well known Cabinet ministers during the Thatcher era. At one point during the 1970s, one Conservative MP, I can't recall who, asked me whether I would consider standing for a seat at the general election (I can't confidently recall which one, but perhaps 1979). Having had some experience of the hardships of the campaign trail when I was Billy McLean's mobile agent, and being reluctant to forsake my career in the City, I decided that the political path was not for me and declined the invitation. I think this was probably for the best – I don't think I would ever have been compliant enough to rigidly follow any party's line and I would have more likely spent more of my time in the Palace of Westminster being ticked off by the chief whip than I would have earnestly representing the views of my constituents.

To my delight, Clarendon became a more regular shooting destination during this period. My cousin, Andrew Christie-

A Clarendon game card. One of many such souvenirs I have kept over the years.

Miller, put a great deal of effort into improving Clarendon's drives and it was always a pleasure to go down there. Further north, I shot regularly at Helmsley in Yorkshire, one of the most famous high pheasant shoots in the country. The estate belonged to Lord Feversham who let out the shoot and I was invited there often by some very interesting people. Among these was Henry Ford II, chairman and chief executive officer of the Ford Motor Company and the eldest grandson of the founder of the company. I first met Henry in Biarritz in about 1960. I was taking a short break there and, one evening, while playing the tables at the casino with four very entertaining Americans, I was invited to join them on the golf course the following day. It was only as we were teeing off that I learned that Henry was one of them and over the ensuing eighteen holes we got on very well and soon became good friends. Henry bought a house near Henley and spent a lot of time in London. Whenever he took the shoot at Helmsley, Henry would hire a very comfortable bus, replete with a well-stocked bar and other luxuries, to take his guests on the journey from London up the M1.

Helmsley was always in great demand and I was fortunate to be invited there by a number of other friends, including Harry Ashcombe and Stas Radziwill. Stas hosted a particularly memorable three days there over the New Year of 1976. Our party included Henry, Harry, Sir Charles Clore, the owner of Lewis's department stores (including Selfridges), and two other great friends, David Metcalfe and John Bodie who also took the shoot at Helmsley frequently. In my game book, I describe the first day of a wonderful stay, New Year's Eve, as 'A remarkable day's shooting even by Helmsley's standards.' The next was no less enjoyable, even after seeing in the New Year in grand style, while the third was a little more difficult following heavy snowfall.

Among those with whom I shot at Helmsley were Sir Charles (later Lord) Forte and his son Rocco. Sir Charles had pioneered the motorway service station and established a very successful hotel empire. Both Rocco and Sir Charles became friends of mine during the seventies and they each shared my love of shooting. I shot with both father and son at Charles' country home, Ryde Farm near Ripley in Surrey. Every occasion was enormous fun and I met some very interesting people there. That is the wonderful thing about the sport: not only did it afford me the opportunity to travel widely across the country and, occasionally, overseas but it also brought me into contact with countless fascinating characters many of whom became dear friends. Throughout life it is often the case that friends come and go as one's circumstances change; I have been most fortunate to have so many friends who have remained close to me through these changes and on whom I can depend utterly.

My club, White's, played a very important part in my life and was a hub where I would meet many of my friends. White's, established in 1693 by the Italian, Francesco Bianco as a hot chocolate emporium, is the oldest and one of the most exclusive gentleman's clubs in London which still upholds its rule of refusing to admit ladies. This tradition caused a stir in 2008 when membership of an exclusively male club was deemed politically incorrect for the then leader of the opposition, David Cameron, who resigned his membership. Cameron's father, Ian, for many years a colleague of mine at Panmure had previously been a chairman of the club. White's was the hub of my social life in London where I would meet with friends and make new ones. For many years I played an active role in the life of the club and sat on various committees and also served as a trustee.

Another sport I briefly became involved with from the early to mid-seventies was horse racing. Ever since my sister, Anne, married Tom Egerton I had been fairly close to the sport and as a regular visitor to Head's Farm I became ever more familiar with how racing operated. It also appealed to my competitive nature and sense of fun; I had always enjoyed a day at the races and for many years and had gone regularly to Newbury, Ascot and other courses. Over a period of some years from the mid-1970s to the early eighties, I owned three horses and enjoyed a little success with them. The first was called *Peterhead*, a *King's Bench* colt, trained by Freddie Maxwell who had a small but relatively successful yard at Lambourn. First time out, *Peterhead* was ridden by no other than Lester Piggott who was then at the peak of his powers. Few horses win on their first run which is primarily aimed at getting them used to racecourse conditions, but Piggott saw enough potential in *Peterhead* to remark that he would like to ride the horse again. At that time, Piggott was stable jockey to Sir Noel Murless and, when the horse was sent out again, at Newbury, Piggott couldn't get off a Murless horse to ride mine. Another great jockey of that period, Greville Starkey, took the ride on *Peterhead* instead. The horse ran well and, having got its nose in front in the final half furlong, looked like it might win. Then, no more than a hundred yards from the line, it suffered a broken leg at full speed. I knew immediately what had happened and as soon as the other horses had passed the post I ran down the course to attend to mine. As so often when a horse breaks a leg, there was absolutely nothing whatsoever that the vet could do for *Peterhead* and he put the horse to sleep with a single shot. It was all very distressing. Having run a hundred yards or so of the course myself, it was little wonder that such an accident should have happened: the ground was hard and in a shocking state, rutted and pitted with holes.

Later, I bought another horse, from Maxwell, called *Regular*, which won a couple of low grade races but which never showed any real promise at a higher level. The third, which I part-owned, briefly showed altogether more potential. I bought a twenty per cent share in a horse called *The Quiet Don*; my friend, John Bodie who had a number of horses owned the other eighty per cent. The 'Don' in the horse's name had Russian rather than Italian connections and he was a grandson of the great *Nijinsky*, which as a three year old in 1970 became the first horse in thirty-five years to win the English Triple Crown of the 2,000 Guineas, The Derby and the St Leger. The feat hasn't been repeated since. With such a fine pedigree we had high hopes for *The Quiet Don* and, initially, as a two year old he didn't disappoint. Trained by Guy Harwood, he was originally a miler who won his each of his first three outings on varying ground in the summer of 1982. The first of these was at Salisbury where he outstayed his rivals on soft ground to win won the Shrewton Maiden Stakes under Greville Starkey at odds of 7-2. This performance caught the eye of a journalist at the *Racing Guardian* who wrote that the horse 'made a favourable impression and looks a useful stayer.' *The Quiet Don* followed up his maiden victory with a second win on the good somewhere in the Midlands and then completed his hat-trick on rattling hard ground at Brighton. I made time in my schedule to see all three races. I particularly remember the Brighton race because it really was a flying visit to the course. I left the office and caught a train, lighting a cigar on the way. I just reached the course in time to see the race and, after seeing *The Quiet Don* outstay the rest of the field and having been presented with the owner's trophy, I was soon back on a London-bound train, puffing away on the same cigar. I was back in the office in no time at all.

Having won in all conditions, Harwood and the team were becoming very excited about the horse's prospects. Though perhaps not a Classics horse, we thought it might enjoy success in good grade races or even in Listed company. To the great disappointment of all *The Quiet Don's* connections, however, its next race was to be its last. It was entered into a race at Thirsk in August and I was unable to get to the track to watch it because I was away shooting grouse somewhere. I begged time off from the afternoon drive to watch the race and settled down in an armchair in front of a television in the gamekeeper's cottage. Immediately, I noticed with alarm that *The Quiet Don* looked simply awful in the paddock and I'm sure that if his trainer had been there the horse would have been withdrawn; unfortunately Guy was away in America looking at horses. My concerns only grew as the horse cantered awkwardly down to the post. It was top weight and a hot favourite in a class of race still well below that which we hoped it would one day reach. My fears were confirmed during the race itself. *The Quiet Don* never looked like winning and eventually trailed in last. It later transpired that the horse had been doped, though by whom remained a mystery. It never ran again and eventually had to be put down. Though I still enjoy and follow the sport and the occasional punt, my racing colours have long since been retired.

Greville Starkey takes *The Quiet Don* to post at Salisbury.

After my divorce from Susie had gone through, I settled down to life as a single man again and, as with all periods of upheaval during one's life, keeping busy and the companionship of friends, colleagues and support from my family helped me through. Then Kim Dearden came into my life. We first met in 1978 at a dinner party in London. I had rushed there from a day's shooting in Yorkshire and she made an immediate impression upon me. She is my second cousin once removed and though I knew of her, we had never previously met – the Cobbold family is inestimably large and it would be impossible to meet all of one's kinsfolk during a single lifetime. Kim's mother was Ann Verity Gibson-Watt whose maternal grandmother was Adela Mary Lucy Cobbold (1865-1921); Adela was an older sister of my grandfather, Ralph Patteson Cobbold. A further link between Cobbolds and Gibson-Watts was made when Kim's aunt, Patricia Gibson-Watt married Robert Nevill Cobbold in 1935. Robert was the son of Philip Wyndham Cobbold, Ralph Patteson Cobbold's youngest brother. Robert was killed in action in Italy during the Second World War. Kim hailed from Hay-on Wye. Her father, Dr Harold Dearden (1883-1961), led a fascinating life, serving as a medical officer on the front line during the First World War before setting up practice as a psychiatrist. He settled his family at Wyecliff on the banks of the river. When the neighbouring property, Net House which had fallen into disrepair, was

Kim with her faithful and supremely clever dog, Muffin.

threatened with demolition, Kim's mother bought it for just £50. It was a sound investment and it remains in the family. From a dilapidated two bedroom cottage, Kim and I have modernised and extended the house. It now has four bedrooms and over the years we have spent many happy weekends there with family and friends. We don't go there so often now, but, with an unobstructed view of the river, it is very popular as a holiday let.

Kim, some years my junior, was working in London in PR and during the course of the dinner party we hit it off very well indeed. We saw each other again shortly afterwards and very soon became inseparable. We had, and still have, much in common, including a mutual love of the countryside and country pursuits and, of course, children. In 1980, I moved out of Vicarage Gardens and we bought a house together just south of the river in Soudan Road, Battersea, in the shadow of the power station. In October of the same year we married. It was quite simply the best thing I ever did. We spent a fabulous honeymoon on Bali. The island really is a paradise and we spent long lazy days on its beaches. One day I tried my hand at boatbuilding, helping some locals who were employing their craft on the shoreline and, on another occasion, Kim and I went to see a cock fight. I can't say we particularly enjoyed the sport but it was certainly interesting in a cultural way. We took our seats towards the top of the steep-sided arena and watched on transfixed not only by the fight itself but also by the animated scene surrounding the cocks as the Balinese cheered on their champions. Perhaps most memorable of all were the clouds of marijuana smoke which wafted up towards our vantage point. By the end of the evening, I think we were almost as high as the locals actually smoking the stuff.

Paradise found. Relaxing on honeymoon in Bali.

Kim came as part of a package. Her dog, Muffin, moved in to Soudan Road with us. He was a mongrel and Kim found him wandering the streets of London as a stray and took him to the local police station. After a week or two, when no one had claimed him, she adopted him. He was an incredible dog with a sixth sense that instinctively seemed to know exactly what was going on. One evening, about a week after we had moved into Soudan Road, I was dining at White's when I received a telephone call from Kim. She was terribly upset. She was visiting friends in North Fulham and Muffin had escaped out the front door. She had combed the surrounding streets but Muffin was nowhere to be found. All searches of the area yielded nothing and as we returned home we began to resign ourselves to never seeing him again. After a distressing night, however, Muffin miraculously appeared on our doorstep at 7 o'clock the next morning, having walked some distance and having crossed the river. This feat was all the more incredible because, having moved to Battersea so recently, Muffin had but little chance to familiarise himself with his new surroundings. How he managed to find his way home remains a mystery to us to this day.

I would often take Muffin with me if I was going shooting and he would get very excited whenever he saw me in my plus fours. The day after his long journey home, I went off shooting somewhere and took Muffin with me. He was such a good companion that I would always take him with me if I could. The following day I was due to shoot at Bowood, somewhere I wasn't able to take him. I told him so, though I didn't expect him to understand. He did. As I donned my shooting clothes and got ready to leave, his usual excitement was replaced with despair. He just lay at the top of the stairs with his head resting on his paws with a very forlorn look in his eyes. Somehow he just knew that he wasn't allowed to come. Over the years, I have had several dogs, all of whom have been faithful and great companions: none were as intelligent as Muffin.

It would be some years before Kim and I had children and during the early eighties we both worked hard in London and enjoyed weekends either at Buckhill or staying with friends or family. Kim was doing very well in PR and, once, I was able to help her to make something of a coup. One evening we were dining with my old friend, Henry Cotton in London. It so happened that Kim had organised a golfing event for a client the following day and I asked Henry if he might be free to attend. He agreed and, though I wasn't present to see it, his appearance unannounced made the day. Kim's corporate clients all turned up suitably attired in Pringle sweaters and golfing slacks and the day began with a driving competition. Each of the assembled party strained every sinew in his attempt to outdrive his colleagues and then Henry, in his seventies by this time, shuffled out of the crowd, dressed not in golfing clothes but in an ordinary suit and took his stance at the tee. Few, if any, of Kim's clients recognised Henry whose heyday was before the Second World War, and so there was universal amazement when he drove his ball straight down the fairway and far beyond the drives of the others. As mouths gaped open, Kim introduced Henry to her clients who were, for the rest of the day, in awe of the great champion. It all made for a very successful day and Kim's clients were not a little impressed that she had managed to secure the services of a true legend of the game.

During this period of my life I became very good friends with John King (later Baron King of Wartnaby). I became friends with him while he was chairman of Babcock International, primarily as a regular shooting companion. I remember shooting with him at Haddon Hall in Derbyshire in early January 1979 just a few days after he had been awarded a Knighthood in the Queen's New Year's Honours list. In 1981 he became chairman of British Airways with the seemingly impossible task of reviving the ailing flagship airline's fortunes. I remember him asking me whether he should accept the offer and I said that he should, but that he should try to gain control of the British Airports Authority (BAA) as well. The BAA owned many of the UK's airports, including Heathrow, and I expressed my concern that if its staff

The Middle Years

went on strike it would be carriers such as BA which would be blamed, quite unfairly, for the disruption. If BA took control of land facilities this risk could be minimised. John tried for BAA but didn't get it. My concerns have been realised since on more than one occasion, most notably in 2008 when BA chairman Willie Walsh blamed BAA for the fiasco surrounding the opening of Heathrow's Terminal 5. BA certainly bore the brunt of traveller disaffection as thousands of bags and cases went missing as Terminal 5's baggage handling system broke down and more than five hundred flights were cancelled.

At the time of John's arrival at BA, the state-owned operator was making an annual loss in excess of £140 million. Within two years, through streamlining, cuts in staffing, axing unprofitable routes and restructuring the board, John had returned the business to profit. This turnaround and BA's subsequent successes have become part of the folklore of the Thatcher era and when BA was floated on the Stock Exchange in 1987 its shares were massively oversubscribed. John has often been described as 'Mrs Thatcher's favourite businessman.'

One area John quickly turned his attention to was BA's aging fleet of aircraft. At that time, BA bought exclusively from Boeing and, in 1982, John very kindly invited Kim and me to join him and his wife, Isabel, on a trip to Boeing's headquarters in Seattle. The purpose of the trip was to look at Boeing's new 757 airliner with a view to placing a large order. As BA was potentially the first global partner for the 757, we were entertained royally. I went purely as John's guest and in no professional capacity. It was all terribly interesting and we were given a full tour of the hangers where any number of jets were being built. In one, there was a 747 Jumbo Jet, which was complete but which hadn't been painted in BA livery or named yet. One of the Boeing executives escorting us on the tour asked me if I would care to name it. I said that I'd be delighted to and quickly tried to come up with something suitable. Though the practice has long since stopped, in those days, all BA aircraft were given a name. There were several themes for these names, themes which conveyed Britishness. For example, planes were named after British cities, islands, lakes or rivers. The theme at the time of our visit was castles, Tintagel, Winchester, Kenilworth, Harlech and Stirling, being among those honoured. Knowing this to be the current convention and mindful that the plane to be christened was a Jumbo Jet, I suggested that *Elephant & Castle,* would be fitting. For many years afterwards whenever I saw the distinctive shape of a Jumbo overhead, I couldn't help wondering if it might be 'mine.' As it happened, sadly I think my idea was not adopted as BA records show no sign of a 747 named *Elephant & Castle* ever having taken to the air.

After a very comfortable few days in Seattle, Boeing laid on a special treat for us. We were flown, by Boeing private jet of course, to Alaska where we spent a week fishing while being put up in the Boeing yacht, *Daedalus.* This was sumptuously furnished and reserved for Boeing top brass and for entertaining customers. John, Isabel, Kim and I were entertained by two senior executives and looked after by four or five crewmen. We wanted for nothing. It must have been some time during the summer because I don't remember it being especially cold. Every day we would set out from the yacht in little motor boats, one couple in each, to fish. I remember once, the tranquillity of the seawater

The Middle Years

lake we were fishing in was shattered by the crack of a gunshot. Startled, I looked round to John and Isabel's boat to see that John had just landed an enormous halibut. It was so large, in fact, that he had been unable to kill it in the conventional way and his boatman had had to resort to pulling a pistol from his pocket and shooting it through the head. Our time in Alaska was unforgettable. It is one of the world's last remaining great wildernesses and it almost felt as if we were its first visitors. We saw killer whales and bears and the scenery was simply beautiful.

For several years in a row, I went with John to both the Farnborough Air Show and the Paris Air Show, which

John and Isabel King with a very large halibut.

were always great fun. Among the most memorable experiences I had in his company occurred when I was given the opportunity to step inside the cockpit of Concorde. John and I were flying together back to London from Washington and had just taken our seats at the very front of the cabin when John, remembering that I had once been a keen flier, asked me if I would like to join the pilot. Of course, I said that I would, and I went into the cramped cockpit, took the jump seat immediately behind the pilot and put a headset on. I listened in to the instructions from the control tower as we taxied to the runway and I remained in the cockpit for takeoff, watching the nose of Concorde rise as we gained altitude. After we had broken the sound barrier, I returned to my seat but later was very kindly invited back by the captain to sit in for landing. It was fascinating and something, I suppose, that very few people have done. Certainly today, in the wake of the atrocities committed on 11 September 2001, no passengers on any airline are allowed anywhere near the cockpit.

Though I never acted on behalf of British Airways, John would sometimes seek my opinion as a friend. At the time when BA was being prepared for privatisation, for example, I recommended he use Rowe & Pitman where my brother-in-law, Peter Wilmot-Sitwell was the senior partner. Some time earlier, I had also suggested to him that having only one supplier of planes, Boeing, was unhealthy for the business and that introducing some competition into this particular supply chain could only benefit BA. I am sure that I was not the only one of his friends or colleagues to make such a recommendation and I am sure that John knew this himself. In April 1984, not long after we had had this conversation, I suggested to John that he should visit Airbus in Toulouse and enter into talks with the company. He agreed and asked me to go with him. We decided to make a short break of it, again taking Kim and Isabel. We took a British Airways private plane, appropriately named Kingair, first to Geneva, where I had arranged a lunch meeting with a banker and, from there, to Venice where we spent a very pleasant two or three days. The trip preceded my 50th birthday by a few days and Kim arranged a surprise for me. Daška, my eldest daughter had just turned twenty-four and as a birthday present, Kim had bought her a ticket to Venice to coincide with our trip. I hadn't been told of this. John, Isabel, Kim and I were sitting in St Mark's Square one day having a drink, when Daška strolled up carrying a copy of the *Financial Times*. It was a lovely surprise.

A lovely surprise. With Daška in Venice.

Eventually, it was down to business in Toulouse, where we stayed for two days and where, just as we had been in Seattle, we were treated like kings. Discussions went well and just before we were due to leave we were having a fine lunch with our hosts. It might well have turned out to be our last lunch altogether. The entire Airbus board had been wheeled in to give us a send-off, and while we were enjoying the hospitality someone entered the room looking rather perturbed. This man explained the problem to the chairman of Airbus, Jean Pierson, in his native tongue, hoping, I am sure, that we, as guests, wouldn't be able to understand what he was saying. Having spent a considerable amount of time in France as a young man however, I was able to follow the gist of the conversation even though it was being conducted in hushed tones and I was sitting two or three places away from Jean. I certainly caught enough to learn that the Airbus ground crew had filled the British Airways private plane with the wrong kind of aviation fuel. Fortunately our pilot had noticed the error, otherwise our engines would have packed up very shortly after takeoff. One can only imagine the headline 'Airbus error kills BA Chairman' and the subsequent damage to Airbus' reputation which was averted by a very narrow margin. Only the eagle eyes of our pilot had saved me from a third (and probably fatal) air accident. Our hosts were a little shamefaced and lent us one of their own small jets to get us home. Our pilot stayed in Toulouse making sure that the tanks of the BA plane were drained properly before he followed us, passengerless, the following day.

By this time, I had had a couple of changes in career. During the early 1980s, Panmure Gordon was going through a difficult time. The two senior partners in the company were both suffering ill health and this began to leave the company rudderless, creating a vacuum at the top of the business which needed to be filled. There were a number of us who could have stepped up; all long-serving partners in our forties. I have always considered my strengths to be in generating business rather than one who defines high level strategy or as one who hires, fires and pays people. This being the case, I ruled myself out of the top job and was not entirely convinced that all of the other candidates were right for the position. I received a number of offers from other companies during this period, but the one which appealed to me more than any other was from the French merchant bank, Worms. Worms focused on corporate banking and the offer made by its head, Nicholas Worms, was very enticing. He told me that Worms' English heritage stretched back nearly one hundred and fifty years and that for most of that time it had had offices in London. These had closed briefly during the Franco-Prussian War and then again for the duration of the First World War. After each conflict, Worms had re-opened its London offices. The Second World War brought about a third closure, but after 1945, the company, for whatever reason, had decided not to recommence its activities in the City of London. Nicholas told me that it was high time that this was set straight and asked me if I would like to set up the operation. He told me that if I wanted to spend £10 million, I could go ahead: if I wanted to spend £20 million, I would have to make a very good case.

It seemed the perfect opportunity; I would be working with a great deal of autonomy for a well-established merchant bank with a proud tradition. However, it would turn out to be a decision which I would regret. Though I went to great efforts to lay the groundwork for some very significant deals, involving companies such as Lazards, Hill Samuel and Rowe & Pitman, when it came to the crunch I received no support whatsoever from Nicholas Worms. For example, Rowe & Pitman were looking for three investors, one from America, one from South Africa and one from Europe. I arranged for Nicholas to go to South Africa to meet with one of the potential investors, Anglo-American, to discuss the matter but Nicholas refused to go. This was by no means an isolated occurrence and, each time something similar happened, it served to undermine my authority and dent my reputation. Over time it became clear to me that my position with Worms was untenable and I left. The years I spent with Worms were undoubtedly the most frustrating of my working life. As my son, Robert (born in 1991) was growing up, I imparted some advice to him; I told him that there are three things that ought to be made illegal – chewing gum, drinking lager beer and working for the French. I would be reasonably confident that he eschewed two of these vulgarisms, though I couldn't be absolutely sure that he survived three years at Bristol University without sampling lager.

I left Worms in the mid-1980s. This marked a crossroads in my career and though I remained in the City, I branched out in a completely new direction. Executive search, or headhunting, was a relatively new industry in the mid-eighties but one which was gaining considerable momentum. The days when one stayed with the same firm for many years were coming to an end and the market was right for professional companies able to bring together the City's brightest individuals and those seeking to recruit. With nearly thirty years' experience of the Square Mile and with a wide network of contacts, I felt I was qualified to give headhunting a go.

6. Headhunting and Slowing Down

During the few years I had been with Worms, I embarked upon a personal side venture which, for a while, did rather well. I had always been interested in oil and for many years had been a non-executive director of the Exploration Company of Louisiana. In the early 1980s, I decided to venture into oil in a more direct way. I set up a company called Energy Recovery Investment Corporation (ERIC), roped in a number of financial institutions, including Worms, to back me and began to invest in oil exploration all around the world. ERIC served purely to back those looking for oil and did not look for or drill for oil itself. Initially the venture was a great success. Indeed, things were going so well that I began to consider bidding for two other medium sized oil companies, Goal and Premier. Had I acquired these targets, ERIC would have become one of the largest oil companies in the UK.

At the time I set up ERIC, oil prices had made a full recovery from the crash of the mid-seventies, peaking at $35 per barrel in 1980. My business rode on this wave until 1986 when the price crashed again, plummeting from $27 to less than $10. Unfortunately this came just at the time I was looking to acquire Goal and Premier. Instead of finding myself bidding for other companies, ERIC itself soon became the target of acquisition. I was unable to fend off the bid and my brief career as an oil magnate came to an abrupt end.

Disillusioned with Worms, I was approached by a number of companies including a large American merchant bank. I was ready for a change of direction, however, and when I received an appealing offer to join the board of executive search company Wrightson Wood, I immediately thought that this was something I could do and I took little persuading. As in all my appointments, I joined Wrightson Wood as a generator of income rather than as one who defines high level strategy. I enjoyed this new challenge and was able to employ the experience of thirty years in the City to good effect. Certainly, a wide network of contacts is one of the key requirements which make a successful headhunter, but integrity, discretion, imagination and the ability to clearly understand one's clients' needs are all equally important.

Executive search was in its relative infancy during the 1980s, though Wrightson Wood was originally established in 1978. When I started my career in the City in the 1950s, people tended to stay with the same firm for a very long time, sometimes for their entire career. This lack of fluidity in the job market was evidenced by Panmure Gordon's protracted courtship of my services during the early 1960s. People simply didn't hop from job to job in those days as they do now. The eighties was perhaps the watershed during which career-long loyalty to a single employer in the City was replaced by competitive individual ambition to get to the top as quickly as one could by moving between firms. In that sense, I moved into executive search at precisely the right time and the depth of my experience and breadth of my professional network enabled me to hit the ground running.

The essential premise of executive search is to find a suitable candidate to fill a senior position for one's client. My customers would typically supply with briefs for the positions to be filled from which I would draw up full job specifications for their approval. On occasions this might vary considerably from that which the client had originally envisaged. It was important that they and I agreed on the requirements of the position; mismatched expectations would most likely lead to a headhunter presenting candidates whom the client might think totally unsuitable. To prevent this from happening, for example, if the firm in question was looking for a non-executive director, I would speak individually to all of the executive directors to understand what each of them was looking for in a candidate. Often I would venture my own opinions and throw these into the mix as well, sometimes tactfully bringing my clients round to my way of thinking. Such discussions had to be handled delicately. Rarely were the opinions of all directors, if any, identical with one another and this made the identification of viable candidates quite a challenge.

 Having established, one way or another, what my client was looking for, I would go off in search of candidates I thought might be suitable and ready to move. I would write a report on each for my client and a preliminary list might have as many as twenty or so names on it. Through discussions with the client this might typically be whittled down to a shortlist of perhaps four or five. Unless I had received express permission from the client, it was usual not to divulge to the candidates the name of the firm I was acting on behalf of. The entire process required the utmost discretion. The reputations of both client and candidate, not to mention that of the headhunter himself, were at stake if loose talk were to give the game away before any deal was struck. The rewards were considerable. These days the executive search market is extremely competitive and rates for placing executives have been squeezed. When I started out in the business, the typical fee was one third of the successful candidate's annual salary, a third of this figure payable as a sort of signing-on fee. In addition to the financial rewards, I gained great satisfaction from fulfilling the needs of my clients having diligently taken great effort in understanding their requirements and in seeking out someone capable of meeting them.

Though I certainly didn't regret the move into executive search, I didn't stay at Wrightson Wood terribly long. Without going into too much detail, neither I nor a number of my colleagues there were entirely comfortable with the way the company was being run. Having cut my teeth in that line of work, I now felt able to set up my own company with others and, in 1987, four of us resigned from Wrightson Wood to set up Stephenson Cobbold.

At this time, Kim and I were still living in Soudan Road. This location proved to be a great choice. Kim made many young friends in Battersea and we became close to one family in particular – the Fairfaxes, Nick and Puss - she the niece of my old friend, John Cowdray. Their three boys arrived only months before each of our children and Rory and my son Robert are great friends to this day. We would often stay with them in their lovely house in Bembridge on the Isle of Wight and, on one memorable visit there, I managed to break the bank in an evening at vingt-et-un at the Bembridge Sailing Club. My financial success brought the evening to an abrupt end!

We had improved the house at Soudan Road

considerably, extending up a floor, and it was a very comfortable home, albeit with a very small garden. We had waited some time before having children, though family time was not in short supply at weekends when we decamped to Buckhill where we were often joined by Daška, Caroline and Arabella who were now young women beginning to forge their own lives and, when they were over from Australia, by Susannah and Kate. All of my children took to Kim the moment they first met her and despite being a far flung family we have always been very close.

In the years before Kim and I had children together, we took some memorable holidays. We were fortunate that some of our friends had houses in exotic locations and we were sometimes asked to join them. I remember, fondly, lazy days with the Hambros in Nassau and with Dru Montagu who in addition to owning property in Spain also had a house in the Dominican Republic. Photograph albums, compiled and notated by Kim, conjure many happy memories spent in the company of dear friends. On the occasion of my fiftieth birthday, Kim and I, together with Caroline and Arabella, went to the deep south of America. Of course, as a director of the Exploration Company of Louisiana I knew that particular state quite well and combined a little business with leisure while I was there. Indeed, we stayed with a fellow director of the company, William C. Huls and his wife Nancy who were very convivial hosts. One of the highlights of the holiday was a visit to the New Orleans World Exposition which occupied a long stretch of the Mississippi in the city. The star attractions were the Mississippi Aerial River Transit, a cable car which carried visitors over the river, and the Space Shuttle Enterprise. It was all quite interesting, though unfortunately for the civic authorities, a dismal commercial flop. Attendances fell well below expectations and this was due in part to the fact that it coincided with the Los Angeles Olympics. In addition, apart from the aforementioned attractions and a mascot, a pelican named Seymoure D. Fair, there simply were not enough spectacular exhibits to pull in the crowds. The New Orleans Exposition has the dubious distinction of being the only World Expo to declare itself bankrupt *during* its run.

At about the same time as I moved into executive search, Kim and I had two children of our own in quick succession. These were, of course, girls, meaning that I had fathered enough to form my own netball team. Sophie arrived in 1985 and Laura a year later. Kim cut down her work in PR in order to look after the girls and in about 1987 or 1988 we decided to put Soudan Road up for sale. The house had served us well and we have very fond memories of our time there but we decided that Kim should live at Buckhill, a beautiful place to bring up young children and that I should buy a small flat in London where I would spend the working week before heading west to be reunited with my young family every Friday evening.

At this time I was at Stephenson Cobbold and I approached an estate agent with a very clear view of the property I was looking for as my home during the week. At his offices, I drew a line on a map connecting my office, which was at the top of Park Lane opposite Marble Arch, and White's and told the somewhat bemused agent that I would only consider properties on or very close to that line. In the meantime, with Kim at Buckhill and Soudan Road sold, a number of friends very kindly put me up during the week. The estate agent proved he was up to the peculiar task I had set him and eventually telephoned me to let me know he had found somewhere he thought met my requirements. The flat in question was in Balfour Place, just behind Purdey's sporting shop on South Audley Street. The agent arranged for me to view the flat and, after a very brief tour, all seemed in order and I made an offer which was accepted. Immediately afterwards I telephoned Kim to tell her the good news that I had found a perfectly located one bedroom flat. A few days later, Kim came up to London to have a look at the flat for herself and was a little surprised to find that it had not one but two bedrooms. When I had viewed it the family living there was at home and I remembered hearing children playing in one of the rooms. I hadn't bothered to look in that particular room and hadn't realised that it was another bedroom. Suddenly, the deal I had made seemed even better.

For a start-up business, Stephenson Cobbold, of which I became chairman, didn't take long to start making money. The company was lean and did remarkably well in its first year. More good years followed but I wasn't destined to stay with the company long. I disagreed with the other partners over the question of how we should reward ourselves following the company's early successes, advocating a more cautious approach while we consolidated the business. My fellow partners saw things differently and I decided it would be best if I left the company. Despite the difficulties I had encountered during my career in headhunting to date, I enjoyed that line of work enormously and wanted to continue in it.

In the meantime and not long before I left Stephenson Cobbold, I made one final contribution to securing the Cobbold line. In 1991, I eventually proved that I was capable of producing a son, Robert, to the immense excitement of the entire family, not least his seven elder sisters. Even before Robert was born, some of his sisters had started having families of their own. I became a grandfather for the first time in 1987 when Caroline and her husband, John Lewis (who sadly died two years later), had a son, Jack. The following year, Daška and her husband, Timothy Hatton, had a son, Thomas and, the year after that, a daughter Leonora. During the 1990s, more grandchildren arrived at quite a rate. Caroline remarried and had two more children, Flora (1994) and Freddie (1997). Arabella married William Oswald in 1994 and has three daughters, Marina (1996), Lucy (1997) and Lara (1999). William is the son of Sir Michael Oswald, the Queen's racing manager and manager of the Royal Studs. From 1970 until her death in 2002, Sir Michael also managed the Queen Mother's racing interests. The Queen very generously lent us Kensington Palace for the wedding and both she and the Queen Mother attended. It was a wonderful day.

My third position in executive research was with Knight Wendling, a company registered in Germany with a pedigree in mining and metals. Through my experience in those particular fields, I knew Erhard Wendling quite well and together we set up an executive search arm of his business in London in 1992, Knight Wendling Executive Search Ltd. Erhard owned 60% of the business and I owned the remainder. This partnership proved successful. Erhard was instrumental in defining the strategy for the business and took charge of hiring, firing and paying people while, operationally, he left me to my own devices to focus purely on generating business. We continued in this vein until 1998.

Erhard, five or six years my junior, was beginning to take things a little easier across all his business interests, spending more time pursuing his passion for golf. This required someone to fill the void this left at the top and I, as on a number of occasions previously, was reluctant to withdraw from the sharp edge of the business in order to take the helm.

Old habits die hard and during the period I was with Knight Wendling, I brokered a deal between two giants of UK media, one traditional, one modern and technically agile. The former was United News & Media plc (UNM), a long-established publisher of regional newspapers and, from 1985, the owner of Express Newspapers which included the *Daily Express*, the *Sunday Express* and the *Daily Star*. In contrast to these right of centre publications, UNM traced its roots back to 1918, when David Lloyd George rallied wealthy Liberal supporters to establish a newspaper group to rival that of the Conservative Lord Northbrook's *Daily Mail*. The chairman of UNM during the eighties and nineties was Lord Stevens of Ludgate. His acquisition of Express Newspapers came at a time when new technologies were replacing 'hot metal' and when Robert Maxwell and Rupert Murdoch, with the help of legislation passed by Mrs Thatcher, were taking on the hitherto all-powerful print unions. Though Stevens had a rather lower profile than his larger-than-life competitors, he brought the Express titles kicking and screaming into the modern age in much the same way and all three publications enjoyed a renaissance and increased circulation by 1990.

The other party I approached had a much shorter history and was a leading force in more modern media. It was this contrast between the two companies which convinced me that they would fit well together. Mills & Allen International had evolved from a failing money broker, the JH Vavasseur Group, under the stewardship of Clive Hollick (from 1991, Baron Hollick of Notting Hill). Hollick steered the group away from banking and into market research and business information services, significantly acquiring National Opinion Polls (NOP) from the *Daily Mail* in 1989. During the early 1990s, MAI moved into television when its subsidiary, Meridian Broadcasting was awarded the ITV franchise for South and South-East England. It later acquired Anglia Television and became a major shareholder in Yorkshire Television and the new national broadcaster, Channel 5.

Not only did I think that the two businesses would complement each other but I also considered that a merger between UNM and MAI would suit the personal aspirations of the chairman of each. Hollick was in his early fifties and the younger of the two and he was looking to paint on a bigger canvas: Stevens, ten years Hollick's senior, was looking for a polite exit from UNM having turned the business around. That is not to say that either party had considered merging with the other. The deal was purely my suggestion.

The idea came to me in August 1994 and I broached the subject with both Stevens and Hollick. They immediately recognised the merits of my proposal and agreed to meet me together. As both sat in the House of Lords it was initially proposed that we should meet there. This was not a terribly good idea as the House was always bustling and we would surely have been seen and rumours would inevitably have begun to circulate.

In the event, it wasn't until the following July that a meeting between the three of us was convened at Stevens' office at 5 o'clock one warm evening. To start with there was some tension in the room as Stevens and Hollick boxed around one other for ten minutes or so. Then one of them said something which broke the ice, the penny dropped and each realised that their ambitions, both corporate and personal, matched each other's perfectly. Discussions continued until 8 when we had to leave for separate dinner engagements but over the coming weeks and months I would meet with either or both on an almost daily basis.

The merger was announced in February 1996. It was big news and Stevens and Hollick arranged press conference which was packed. After each had delivered a statement to the assembled throng, the floor was opened for questions. 'Did Warburg bring you this idea?' asked one reporter. 'No.' replied David Stevens, 'Nicholas Cobbold did.' I had intended to keep a low profile during the press conference but once Stevens had let the cat out of the bag I found myself in the uneasy position of being pursued by a scrum of reporters and photographers.

The merged group retained the UNM name. Hollick became chief executive while Stevens stayed on as chairman until 1999. During that period and more recently the company has been transformed through a series of acquisitions and divestments. In 2000 it began to focus primarily on business services, encompassing market research, conferences and trade seminars and business publishing, selling its television interests to Granada and Express Newspapers to the Northern & Shell Group. To emphasise this change in approach the group adopted the name United Business Media (UBM). It is, today, the largest company of its kind in the world and, at the time of writing, its chief executive is, coincidentally, Tim Cobbold, a not too distant relative.

Having decided that I didn't want to assume full responsibility for running Knight Wendling Executive Search, I joined Norman Broadbent, a large and well-established company. Norman Broadbent had been courting my services for some time, a courtship not dissimilar to that which had prised me away from Williams de Broë some three decades or so earlier. Some very close friends were among the company's non-executive directors, including John King, Johnny Louden and Duncan McGowan with whom I had worked at Panmure Gordon. Over a period of two or three years, I was approached by all of them separately to join the board as an executive director. At first, much as I had done when approached by Panmure, I resisted the temptation, due mainly to the fact that I didn't feel I would fit in well with one or two of the members of the existing board. Then, with my departure from Knight Wendling imminent, my friends asked me whether I might reconsider joining them if structural changes were made that would overcome my objections. To be precise, I was asked whether I would reconsider if these changes were put in place by 11 o'clock the following day. I said, 'Speak to me in the afternoon.'

I was aware that my friends wanted me to come in to run Norman Broadbent. They were aware that this was unlikely, knowing that I preferred transacting business rather than steering it. My views prevailed and I joined the board. Norman Broadbent was a much larger concern than any of the executive search companies I had been with previously and its diverse client portfolio extended far beyond the confines of the Square Mile. I enjoyed tackling the variety of assignments which came my way and worked not only with financial institutions inside and outside the City of London, but also with mining and oil companies and with government departments. The latter, of course, required absolute discretion. One public office assignment was particularly delicate; so much so that I am still unable to divulge the full details of it today. This government department was seeking a non-executive director and after long discussions with its senior people I went away and drew up an initial shortlist of nineteen names. This was later whittled down to four but not until the very last stage of the assignment was I able to divulge the name of my client to any of the candidates, all of whom were highly credible. The one who got the job proved to be a great success. In connection with this and other work I did in the public sector I was fortunate enough to be awarded an OBE in the Queen's New Year's Honours for 2002. The certificate hangs in the lavatory at my home and bears the citation, 'for public service.'

I was very happy at Norman Broadbent. I was among friends working in an exciting, fast-moving and challenging industry. In one particularly successful year I managed to invoice over £1 million worth of business. I was already in my mid-sixties but felt a new lease of life. I stayed with the company beyond my seventieth birthday and held several non-executive directorships too. Later, when Bruno Pace, a former colleague at Norman Broadbent went out on his own in 2009, I accepted his invitation to become an associate director and in this capacity I have introduced work to him.

Through the autumn of my life, my love of shooting

remained undiminished and I continued to travel long distances in pursuit of its pleasures for as long as I could. Even when the driving became a little too much for me, Kim, whenever she was able, would drive me around; often Sophie, Laura and Robert would come along too. I had been comfortable with a gun in my hand from as far back as I can remember and shooting had been at the heart of my social life for nearly fifty years. Many of the friendships I made on the grouse moors of Scotland or elsewhere in the beautiful countryside of the British Isles have endured for many years.

Sadly though, as the years advance, one has to come to terms with losing many of those with whom wonderful memories have been made. If any one man harnessed my early exuberant interest in the sport and was a constant shooting companion year after year it had been John Cowdray and I felt an immense loss when he passed away in January 1995, aged 84. There was no place I looked forward to visiting more than Dunecht and I have countless fond memories of time spent in John's company. My game book records my last shoot in John's company on 20 December 1990 on his Sussex estate.

John Cowdray.

Along with Dunecht, Dumbleton was another of the great staples in the shooting calendar and it came as a great shock to learn of the sudden death of my cousin and dear friend, Charlie Hambro in early November 2002. Charlie was an outstanding shot who made *The Field's* top hundred and he had an infectious exuberance which made him the perfect host, whether at his Gloucestershire home or at his place in the Bahamas. His obituarist in *The Telegraph* astutely observed,

> Part of his charm stemmed from the manner in which both his hospitality and handling of a gun were made to seem effortless, rather than the fruits of intense painstaking and skill.

Once, while staying in Nassau, Charlie offered a Hambro's cheque to settle an evening's gambling debts at the casino. When he presented it, the disgruntled owner exclaimed that 'we could all print our own cheques if we wanted to.' Charlie left it to one of his friends to explain to the owner what the name Hambro represented in the financial world. John and Charlie are but two of the many dear friends I have lost and, inevitably, the older one gets the more regularly one has to attend the funerals of one's contemporaries.

When I eventually retired from Norman Broadbent not so many years ago, I sold the flat at Balfour Place to a Russian gentleman, making a tidy profit on my original investment. By this time, we had moved out of Buckhill. This was a great shame; I had the house for thirty years and would have kept it for many more had our landlord not decided to give it over to his family.

We were settled in the area and, now that I had retired, I was extremely keen to stay in the rural idyll of the Wiltshire countryside. In the short term, we took Home Farm on Lord Suffolk's Charlton Park estate just outside Malmesbury. Home Farm was very comfortable and we enjoyed our time there, but it was always intended as a stopgap while we looked for somewhere to buy in the area. After about three years or so, we found the perfect place in May 2004. Malthouse Farm appears on maps of the village of Eastcourt as far back as the late seventeenth century, though sadly the Malthouse that once stood on the other side of the lane has long been demolished. The farm now is a home full of character and interesting features with some land, a number of outbuildings and a duck pond. It also has three tied cottages. The house needed quite a lot of work when we moved in. One of the outbuildings housed an indoor swimming pool which we decided to cover over. This building, which we call the long room is glazed floor to ceiling on one side and gets the sun almost all day. Recently, as the stairs in the farmhouse have become more difficult for me, the long room has become my own annexe with bedroom, bathroom, kitchen, living room and office space. The walls are covered with paintings and photographs of the places and people most dear to me. One or two of the compositions which adorn the walls of our home have been painted by me.

One of my paintings.

Headhunting and Slowing Down

Malthouse Farm.

As one gets older, life becomes a little more prosaic. The latter years of my life are perhaps not so peppered with tales of adventure, risk and tomfoolery as the earlier ones, though my freedom of spirit has diminished little. If I could, I would dearly love to have one more crack at the Cresta Run or to take the controls of a helicopter one last time. To one who has always liked the thrill of speed, the slowness which comes with age is particularly frustrating, though I was pushing 70 when I received my very first speeding ticket from the police in Kim's Porsche in which I was doing considerably more than 70 on the M5 on the way back from a shoot somewhere.

As I write this, I am now 80 and although my health has not been all it once was, the old engine is still ticking over. I have been immensely fortunate in my life. Some of my schoolmates did not emerge from the Shobrooke fire; I survived two aircraft accidents, a spectacular crash atop a toboggan and a perilous voyage in a ship with a severe list. Beyond these narrow escapes my life has been charmed in so many ways. I have enjoyed my work and have always, somehow, managed to maintain a healthy and happy balance between career and leisure. Shooting has always been at the centre of my life and now, as I sit in the long room at Malthouse Farm, the occasional crack of a gun I hear in the distance still sets my pulse racing. My love of the sport took me to some very interesting places in Britain and overseas and has provided me with so many happy memories. Above all it gave me a very wide circle of friends and acquaintances, some of whom I simply would never have met otherwise. The number of friends on whom I have been able to depend absolutely and who have been there for me through thick and thin throughout my life is quite extraordinary. Of course, with the passage of time, it becomes a little trickier to meet up with one's friends, but good friendships transcend such difficulties and can be sustained by an occasional letter, telephone call or Christmas card. This said, Malthouse Farm is rarely empty. With a large family and so many good friends, we have a steady stream of visitors.

My children lead busy successful lives. All that a parent can ask is that one's children are happy, healthy and fulfilled and I am most fortunate in this regard. Such is the pace of modern life that it is rare for us all to get together, but I am never happier than when this is possible as on the occasion of my 80th birthday. I took a while building my family; my youngest is thirty years the junior of my eldest. When they were younger, our family set up was never the most straightforward but it has always been immensely gratifying to me that all are so close to one another as well as to me and to Kim. Family gatherings are always tremendous fun, particularly with my grandchildren around and, of course, these days it is so much easier to stay in touch through the wonders of modern communications. Susannah and Kate still live in Australia and at the time of writing Laura is in Madrid; to be able to speak to them face to face on a computer screen (with a little help from Kim on the technical side) is a wonderful thing. I am always eager to hear news from any of my children or, indeed, grandchildren and, with so many, I seldom have to wait long for some. I also hope that I am still able, when asked, to dispense some advice to them which may be worth heeding.

Index

Abyssinia 5, 112
Acrise, Kent (*see* Cobbold, Nicholas, homes)
Aden 114
Ahmad, King of Yemen 98
Air Hanson 127, 151
Airbus 186-8
al-Badr, Mohamed 98, 100, 112, 114
Alan Mann Helicopters 125
Alaska 184-5
Albania 95, 99, 100
Albert, Prince of Monaco 93
Alderbury, Wiltshire 16
Alexandria 72
Allied Breweries 158
Amery, Julian 95
Anglia Television 200
Anglo American 189
Annabel's (London restaurant) 117-8
Aqaba 59
Archie Kidd Ltd. 132-3
Arromanches, Normandy 21
Ascot Racecourse 127, 174
Ashcombe, Harry 154, 173
Atholl, Duke of 106
Atholl estates, Scotland 102, 106
Auster (aeroplane) 67
Australia 168-9, 194, 209
Austria 79
Avallon, France 134
Azay le Rideau, Château 141

Babcock International 182
Badham, Sergeant 73
Bahamas 6
Balcombe, West Sussex 9
Balfour Place (*see* Cobbold, Nicholas, homes)
Bali 179-80
Banac, Božo 82
Banac, Milica 93
Bank of England 61-2
Barber, Alan 33
Baring, Nicholas 64
Barney (horse) 19
Barron, John 71
Bass 158
Basset, Bryan 87
Basset, Carey 87
Bath, 5th Marquess of 28, 29
Bath, 6th Marquess of 30
Bathurst Estate 126
Battersea Heliport 124-5, 126, 132, 134, 138, 140, 142, 144-7
Beaton, Cecil 32
Beatty, David 126
Beaufort, Duke of 27
Beauly, Inverness-shire 108-9
Beauly, River 108-9
Beit, Alfred 5
Bell (helicopters) 124-5, 151
Bell, Emily 39-40
Bellville, Jeremy 42, 44, 76-8, 87-8
Belvoir Castle 78
Bembridge 194

Bembridge Sailing Club 194
Benyon, William 70
Bernese Alps 136-7
Béthune, France 6
Biarritz 123, 130-1
Bietschorn 136-7
Biggin Hill 127
bin Laden, Salem 116
Birkbeck, Caroline 134, 136
Birse Castle 23
Biscay, Bay of 60
Bishop of Salisbury 32
Blackwell, David 134-7, 139
Bland (schoolboy at St Peter's Court) 38-9
Blenheim Palace 102, 106, 121-4
Bodie, John 173
Boeing 183-5
Boer War, Second 7-8
Bordeaux 49-50
Borneo 51-2
Borneo Company Limited 51
Boscombe Down 20
Bousfield, Donald 45
Bowood 166-8, 171, 181
Boys-Stones, Simpson and Spencer 66
Brabham, Jack 90
Bradman, Don 44
Bramwell (chauffeur) 123-4
Brantridge Park 1, 9-10, 86
Brighton Racecourse 176
Brigitte (girlfriend) 117
Bristol Superfreighter (aeroplane) 89

Bristol University 190
Britain, Battle of 20, 21
Britannia Royal Naval College, Dartmouth 55
Britannia Stakes, Royal Ascot 127
British Amateur Golf Championship 4
British Airports Authority 182-3
British Airways 182-6
British Association of Plastic Surgeons 71
Britwell Court 8-9
Brixton prison 83
Broadstairs 34, 42
Brodrick, St. John 5
Brocklehurst, Elizabeth 130
Brocklehurst, Mark 87, 103, 130, 143, 171
Brooke, David 129
Brown, George 118
Bruntisfield, Lord 106
Buckhill House (*see* Cobbold, Nicholas, homes)
Buckingham Palace 61
Burns, George 61, 65, 75
Buxted Park Hotel 127-8

Cairo 58, 60
Calvados region 23
Calvet, Maison 50
Cambridge University 48
   Magdalen College 4
   Peterhouse College 82
Camel Estuary 132
Cameron, David 92, 174

Index

Cameron, Ian 92, 128, 174
Cameron, Mary 128
Campbell (Skye publican) 97
Canada 5-6
Capel, Suffolk 139
Carnarvon, Lord 31
Caroline, Princess of Monaco 93
Caterham 54-5, 56, 165
Cavendish, 9th Duke of 52
Cavendish, Blanche 5
Cavendish Hotel, London 69
Cazenove's 164
Cenotaph, The, London 53
Central Asia 4-5, 112
Central Mining Group 5
Chaddleworth 127, 133, 150
Chambord, Château 141
Channel 5
Charbonnel et Walker 31
Charlesworth, Peter 38
Charlton, Jack 148
Charlton Park 206
Charmaine (motor yacht) 88
Chenonceau, Château 141
Cherbourg 132
Chicheley Hall 126
Christie Miller family 7-8
Christie-Miller, Andrew 111, 171-2
Christie-Miller, Edward 54
Christie-Miller, Michael 11, 20, 23-4, 42, 53, 54
Christie-Miller, Norah Veronica Vandeleur 7, 8, 9, 12, 26, 40, 57, 70-1, 150

Christie-Miller, Sammy 11, 23, 71, 110-1
Christie-Miller, Sydney Richardson 8
Christie's Auction Houses 129
Church Farm, Cirencester 129-30
Churchill, Winston 57, 103
Cirencester 126, 129-30, 151
City of London (see London, City of)
Civil Aviation Authority, The 153
Clare, County 7
Clarendon Park (see Cobbold, Nicolas, homes)
Clore, Charles 173
Coates, Archie 147-8
Coates, Gloucestershire 151
Cobbold, Adela 178
Cobbold, Anne 10, 12, 64, 86, 126-7, 128, 134, 141, 150, 174
Cobbold, Anthony 53
Cobbold, Arabella 111, 125, 138-9, 146-7, 151, 168, 171, 195, 198
Cobbold, Barbara Elizabeth 51
Cobbold, Caroline 93-4, 125, 129, 138-9, 151, 168, 171, 194, 195, 198
Cobbold, Charlotte 43
Cobbold, Clare 10, 12, 64-5, 86, 128, 147
Cobbold, Daška 85, 87, 125, 138-9, 151, 167-8, 171, 186-7, 195, 198
Cobbold, David 53
Cobbold, David Anthony 43

Cobbold, Esther 53
Cobbold, Humphrey 53
Cobbold, Jack 53
Cobbold, Jeremy 53
Cobbold, Jocelyn 129, 138-9
Cobbold, John (b. 1746) 3
Cobbold, John Cavendish 87, 139
Cobbold, John Dupuis 109
Cobbold, John Murray 52, 54
Cobbold, Kate 168-9, 171, 195, 198, 209
Cobbold, Kim (née Dearden) 178-84, 186-7, 194-7, 204, 207-9
Cobbold, Laura 168, 196, 198, 204, 209
Cobbold, Marina (née Kennedy) 81-4, 85, 93-4, 95, 102, 113, 116, 117, 151, 166-8
Cobbold, Nicholas
   career
      Knight Wendling 198-9, 202, 203
      Norman Broadbent 202-3
      Panmure Gordon 92-3, 116, 117, 151, 158-9, 161, 164-6, 174, 188, 202
      Stephenson Cobbold 194, 196-7
      Williams de Broë 65, 67-8, 76, 78, 81, 85, 92-3, 96, 159
      Worms 189-90, 191

Wrightson Wood 192-4
cars
   Alfa Romeo 96-7
   Aston Martin 170
   Bentley 119-20, 170
   Ferrari 275 GTB 170
   Ferrari 400
   Ford Popular 63-4, 67, 89
   Maserati Mistral 170
   Renault Dauphine 90-1, 170
   Wolseley Hornet 56-7
falconry 115
flying
   aeroplanes 66-7, 121
   helicopters 121, 124-44, 149-53
French wine houses, and, 49-51
homes
   Acrise 86-9, 91, 121, 139
   Balfour Place 197, 205
   Buckhill House 166-7, 169, 181, 195, 196, 205
   Clarendon Park 9, 10-23, 26-7, 30-3, 43, 47, 100, 110-1, 147, 171-2
   Hays Mews 85
   Home Farm 206
   Hyde Park Square 85, 91, 94-5
   Malthouse Farm 206-8
   Net House 178-9
   Pont Street 63, 68-9
   Rutland Gate 2, 12, 43

Index

Seymour Walk 94-5, 116, 166, 169
Soudan Road 179, 180-1, 194-5, 196
Vicarage Gardens 169, 179, 180-1
horse racing 115, 141, 174-7
National Service 48, 49, 54-65
OBE 203
photographs of 1, 12, 16, 19, 26, 47, 65, 83, 104, 110, 115, 125, 133, 139, 146, 157, 180, 187
schooling
    Eton College 43-6
    Ludgrove 33-5
    St Peter's Court 33-42
shooting 18-20, 79, 100-10, 116, 117-8, 120-1, 154-8, 204, 208
winter sports 79-81
Yemen Civil War 112-4
Cobbold, Pamela 110
Cobbold, Patrick 44, 54, 56, 59-60
Cobbold, Peter 51-2
Cobbold, Philip Wyndham 178
Cobbold, Ralph Hamilton 3-4, 12, 25, 26, 42-3, 69, 86, 111-2, 129 138-9, 147, 148
Cobbold, Robert 53, 102. 190, 194, 198, 204
Cobbold, Robert Nevill 178
Cobbold, Sophie 168, 196, 198, 204

Cobbold, Susannah 146-7, 168-9, 171, 195, 198, 209
Cobbold, Thomas 2-3
Cobbold, Tim 53, 202
Cobbold-Sawle, Ralph Patteson 4-7, 95, 99, 111-2, 113, 178
Coe, Bob 10-1
Cognac 50
Coldstream Guards 23, 24, 26, 54, 57
Cole, Horace de Vere 30
Coley, Ian 110
Concorde (aeroplane) 185-6
Connor, Doug 80
Conservative Party 83, 95-6, 171
Cooper, John 90-1
Cooper-Climax (motor racing team) 90
Cortina, Italy 119-20, 170
Côte d'Opale airport, Le Touquet 89
Cotentin Peninsula 131
Cotton, Henry 119, 181-2
Coughton Court 129
Cowdray, John 23, 79, 100-1, 102 107-8, 131, 142, 170, 204-5
Craig, Tom 54
Crawley, Camilla, 12, 26
Crawley, Cosmo 12, 25, 141
Crawley, Henrietta 12, 26
Crawley, Rosemary 10
Crawley, Sarah 12-9, 22, 26-7, 29, 32-3, 42, 86-7, 129, 141
Crediton 35, 38-40
Cresta Run 79-81, 119, 207

Cricket 3-4, 44, 45
Croatia 81
Croydon Airport 54
Cuban Missile Crisis 98
Curzon, Lord 4

D-Day 21-2, 23-4, 26-7, 42, 60
Daedalus (yacht) 184
Daily Express 199-200
Daisy (horse) 15
Dan (whippet) 75
Dearden, Harold 178
Dearden, Kim (*see* Cobbold, Kim)
Dee, River 107-8
Devizes 132
Devon County Council 35
Devonshire, 9th Duke of
Dickin, John 126, 127, 142
Dietz, Howard 131
Digby, Eddie 54
Dijon 134, 136, 140
Dijon Val-Suzon 140
Dixton, Gloucestershire 102, 143
Dominican Republic 195
Donald (Longleat butler) 30
Dorchester Hotel 83
Dorking 150
Dover, Straits of 131
Drinkwater, Peter 74
Dudley, Earl of 9, 106
Dumbleton, Gloucestershire 110, 143, 170, 205
Dummer, Hampshire 69, 147
Dunecht, Aberdeenshire 107-8, 142, 205

Dunkeld, Perthshire 106
Dunkirk 79

Earls Court 62-3
Eastcourt 206-7
Easton Neston 129
Eaton Hall, Cheshire 55-7
Eckstein, Herman 5
Eden, Anthony 72
Edinglassie, Aberdeenshire 107
Edward VII, King 5
Egerton, Anne (*see* Cobbold, Anne)
Egerton, Charles 127
Egerton, Tom 126-7, 128, 134, 141, 150, 174
Egypt 7, 57-60, 72-3, 98-9
El Alamein 40
Elizabeth, Queen, the Queen Mother 198
Elizabeth II, Queen 62-3, 198
Elwes, Dominic 83
Elwes, Simon 83
ERIC (oil company) 191
Ethiopia 159
Eton College 3-4, 13, 34, 43-6, 48, 51, 54, 63, 64, 84, 88
Evening Standard 148-9
Evershot, Dorset 46
Exeter 39, 134
Exploration Company of Louisiana 191, 195
Express Newspapers 199-200, 202
Eyemouth, Berwickshire 150

Index

Fairey Aviation 54
Fairey, Dick 54
Fairfax, Nick 194
Fairfax, Puss 194
Fairfax, Rory 194
Faisal, King of Saudi Arabia 113
Farnborough Air Show 185
Farouk, King of Egypt 57
Fayid, Egypt 58, 60
Fedayeen 58-9
Ferrières, Château de 117-8
Feversham, Lord 172
Field, The 110, 205
Final Chord (racehorse) 127
Financial Times 187
Fitzwilliam family 101-2, 170
Fitzwilliam, Joyce 102, 142
Fitzwilliam, Tom 102, 142
Fives 45
Flanders 52
Fleet Air Arm 76
Flying Fortress (aeroplane) 20
Fonthill 32, 130
Ford II, Henry 172-3
Formula 1 90, 128-9
Formula 2 90
Forte, Charles 173
Forte, Rocco 173
Fortescue, Arthur 57
Fox-Strangways family 32
Fox-Strangways, Giles 33, 46-7
Fox-Strangways, John 25
France 21, 24, 49-51, 72, 88-9, 131, 134-6, 137-8, 139-40, 187-8
Franks, Brian 99

Fraser, Hugh 106
Fraser, Simon 106, 108-9

Gatwick Airport 127, 129, 130-2, 139, 144
Geneva 136, 137, 186
Geneva, Lake 136
George III, King 43
George V, King 35
George VI, King 43, 51
Germany 6, 24, 109
Gibson-Watt, Ann 178-9
Gibson-Watt, Patricia 178
Gironde, River 49
Gloucester Duke of 41
Goal (oil company) 191
Golders Green 111
Golf 4, 43-4, 173, 181-2, 199
Grace, Princess of Monaco 93-4
Granada Television 201
Grand Metropolitan 158
Grant, Flora 198
Grant, Freddie 198
Great Bitter Lake, Egypt 58
Great Mongeham, Kent 44
Grenadier Guards 24, 65
Guards Armoured Brigade 26
Guards Brigade 4th 75
Guards' Chapel, Wellington Barracks 52-3, 54
Guinness, Loel 130
Gurdon, Charlie 39-40
Gurdon, Jeryl 42
Gurdon, Robin 39-40

Haddon Hall 102, 182
Hambro family 110, 195
Hambro, Charlie 110, 126, 141, 143-4, 205
Harrow School 4
Hart-Davis, Duff 100
Harwich 2
Harwood, Guy 175-7
Hatton, Leonora 198
Hatton, Thomas 198
Hatton, Timothy 198
Havana 83
Hay-on-Wye 178-9
Heads Farm, Chaddleworth 127, 128, 132, 150, 174
Heathrow Airport 144, 183
Heidsieck, Charles 50
Heli Air Ltd. 143, 151
Helmsley 172-3
Henderson, Ian 87
Henderson, Sarah (*see* Crawley, Sarah)
Henley 150
Hennessy Cognac 50
Herbert, David 32
Hesketh, Lord 129
Heston Airport 9
High School, The, Crediton 40
Highclere Castle 31
Hill Samuel 189
Hinden, Jack 8
Hohenlohe, Alfonso 117
Hollick, Clive 200-2
Hollies, Eric 44
Holywells, Ipswich 3

Home Farm (*see* Cobbold, Nicholas, homes)
Home, Lord 99
Horse Racing 115, 127, 141, 174-7, 199
Houghton 102
House of Commons 72, 98, 171
House of Lords 200
Huls, Nancy 195
Huls, William 195
Hunt, James 129
Huntley & Palmers 132-3
Hurst Park Racecourse 95
Hyde Park Square, London (*see* Cobbold, Nicholas, homes)

India 4-5, 99
Inverness 96-8
Ipswich 2-3
Ipswich Town Football Club 52, 139
Irish Guards 7, 159
Isle of Skye 97
Isle of Wight 76, 131, 194
Israel 99
Issigonis, Alec 90
Italy 119-20, 178
Ivanović, Ivan 81-2
Ivanović-Banać, Daška 81, 87

Jamaica 123
James, Arthur 65
Japanese Imperial Army 51-2
Jeddah 113
Jeffrey, Edith 69

Index

JH Vavasseur Group 200
Jo (girlfriend) 159-61, 164
Johnson, Jim 100, 112
Johnstone, Johnny 144-5
Johnstone, Russell 97-8
Jordan 99
Juno Beach, Normandy 60
Justerini & Brooks 3, 43

Karakoram Mountains 95
Kashgar 95
Keeling (Nanny) 12
Kennedy, Geoffrey 82
Kennedy, Marina (*see* Cobbold, Marina)
Kennedy, Tessa 82-3
Kensington Palace 198
Kent, Duke of 41
Kenya 154-8
Kidlington, Oxfordshire 121
Kilamoy (Masai guide) 156
Kilrush, County Clare 7
King, Isabel 183, 185-7
King, John 182-8, 202
King's Bench (racehorse) 174
Kipper (pupil at Solent Road School) 17-8
Kirkland Lake, Ontario 6
Kitchener, Herbert Horatio 7
Klosters 125
Knight Wendling (*see* Cobbold, Nicholas, career)
Knipe, Elizabeth 3
Korean War 57, 76
Krug, Paul 50

Labour Party 95
Lambeth Palace 159-64
Lamington, South Lanarks 141
Lancashire, HMTS 60-1
Lansdowne, 5th Marquess of 5
Lazards 189
Le Mans 24 Hour Race 90
Le Touquet-Paris-Plage 88-9, 121 135-6, 138, 139-40
Leadhills 141-2, 150
Lesley-Melville family 141
Lewis, Jack 198
Lewis, John 198
Lewis, Rosa 69
Life Guards 63
Lindsay, Patrick 129
Linlithgow, Lord 141
Liverpool 61
Livingstone (St Peter's Court schoolboy) 40
Lloyd George, David 199
Lloyds of London 100
Loire Valley 137, 140
Lola (tenant Pont Street) 68-9
London 7, 9, 10, 53, 61-3, 67-9, 83, 85, 94-5, 111, 144-7, 148-50, 166, 168, 174, 178, 179-81, 185 196-7
London, City of 65-6, 84, 124, 151, 189-90, 203
London Radar 134
Londonderry, Lord 103
Long Nawang, Borneo 51
Long Range Desert Group 40
Longbridge Deverill 26

Longford Castle 32
Longleat 27-30, 130
Lord, John Clifford 24
Los Angeles Olympics 195
Lötschental Valley 136
Loudon, Johnny 119, 202
Lovat, Shimi (*see* Fraser, Simon)
Lower Saxony 24
Lucan, Lord 83
Ludgrove School 33-5, 44, 45, 102
Lumley, Richard 44
Lydd Airport 89
Lympne Airport 89

MacDermott, Brian 159-66
Macmillan, Harold 9, 99
Mad Mullah, The 5
Madrid 209
Magdalen College, Oxford
    (*see* Oxford University)
Magdalene College, Cambridge
    (*see* Cambridge University)
Maidenhead 67
Mallaig 97
Malmesbury 206
Malta 58
Malthouse Farm (*see* Cobbold, Nicholas, homes)
Manton family 102
Manton, Mimi 102
Marbella 117
Marchmont, Berwickshire 110
Marlborough, Duke of 106, 121-4
Marlow 44, 57, 64-5, 69, 150
Mary, Queen 42

Masai Mara 154-8
Maxse, Frederick Ivor 8
Maxwell, Freddie 174-5
Maxwell, John Grenfell 5
Maxwell Robert 199
Mayhew, David 165
MCC 4
McCann, Mr (Latin tutor) 33
McEwen family 110
McEwen, Alexander 119-20, 129, 150
McEwen, Cecilia 129
McEwen, David 103
McEwen, John 103
McEwen, Robin 103
McGowan, Duncan 202
McKinley Wilson, Susie 127, 129-30, 132-4, 136, 138-41, 144, 146, 150-1, 154-6, 166, 168-9, 177
McLean, Alexander 97
McLean, Neil 'Billy' 82, 95-8, 99-100, 112-3, 171
Melbourne 126
Melbury 32, 46
Menelik II 5
Mercer, Joe 127
Meridian Broadcasting 200
Merrylegs (horse) 15
Messerschmitt (aeroplane) 21
Metcalfe, David 173
Miami 83
Midsomer Norton 26
Miglietta, Adriano 131
Migron, Domaine de 130-2

Index

Miller, William Henry 8
Mills & Allen International 200-1
Milton 102, 142
Ministry of War Transport 82
Mississippi River 195
Monaco 82, 93
Montagu, Dru 109, 195
Monte Carlo 83, 93-4
Montreuil 135
Morocco 118
Morrison family 32
Morrison, Charles 32
Morrison, James 32
Mosquito (aeroplane) 20
Motor Racing 128-9
Mouland, Jim 12, 22
Mountfield, Sussex 126
Mouton Rothschild, Château 49
Muffin (dog) 180-1
Murdoch, Rupert 199
Murless, Noel 175

Nantclwyd, Wales 89, 110, 170
Nantes 131-2
Nassau 195, 205
Nasser, General 72, 98-9, 112, 114
National Geographic 83
National Opinion Polls 200
Naylor-Leyland, Jakes 130
Naylor-Leyland, Michael 126, 130, 151-2
Naylor-Leyland, Vivyan 89, 110
Neguib, General 57
Net House (*see* Cobbold, Nicholas, homes)

New England, Newmarket 105
New Orleans 195-6
New York 83
Newbury 127
Newbury Racecourse 115, 141, 174-5
Newcastle Airport 66-7
Newcastle upon Tyne 66-7
Newport Pagnall 126
Newquay 133
Newton Ferrers, Devon 88
Nigeria 7
Nijinsky (racehorse) 175
Nile Valley 159
Norman Broadbent (*see* Cobbold, Nicholas, career)
Normanby Hall 102
Normandy 21, 23, 24, 27
Northbrook, Lord 200
Northern & Shell 201
Northern Counties Club 66
Nuer (tribe) 159
Nylstroom, South Africa 7

Oakes, Harry 6
Odstock Hospital, Salisbury 71
Old Sarum 20, 127
Omdurman, Battle of 7
Ontario 6
OPEC 153, 158
Open Golf Championship 119
Opéra de Monte Carlo 93-4
Orford, Suffolk 129, 138-9
Orléans 137-8, 140
Orwell, River 2

Osijek, Croatia 81
Ostend 120, 170
Oswald, Lara 198
Oswald, Lucy 198
Oswald, Marina 198
Oswald, Michael 198
Oswald, William 198
Ox and Bucks Light Infantry 6
Oxford 170
Oxford University 48
    Magdalen College 10

Pace, Bruno 203
Panmure Gordon (*see* Cobbold,
    Nicholas, career)
Parachute Brigade, 1st 24
Paris 50
Paris Air Show 185
Parker, Mrs (Longleat
    housekeeper) 29-30
Pauillac, Médoc 49-50
Pembroke, Lord 110
Penhale Sands 133-4
Penrice House, Porthpean 7, 111
Perranporth 133
Personal Service League 13
Perth, Australia 168
Peterhead (racehorse) 174-5
Peterson, Jack 33-4, 45
Petra 59
Phillips, Tanis 130-2
Phillips, Teddy 130-2
Pickering Camp 74-5
Pierre, Prince of Monaco 93
Pierson, Jean 187-8

Piggott, Lester 174-5
Piper's Farm 18
Pirbright Camp 25, 73-4
Pitt, Minnie Diana 5
Plessey 143, 153
Polzeath 132-4
Pompidou, Georges 117-8
Port Said 59
Portsmouth 17, 20, 21
Poseidon NL (mining company)
    124
Premier (oil company) 191
Preston 95
Prestwick Golf Club 4
Pretoria 5, 8
Prim (air hostess) 67
Purdey's 196

Queen Charlotte Hospital,
    Hammersmith 85
Queen Elizabeth Grammar
    School, Crediton 40

Racing Guardian 176
Radnor Family 31-2
Radziwill, Stanislaw 154, 173
Rainier III, Prince 82, 93
Rawlings, Patricia 129
Reading Battle Hospital 70-1
Red Cross, The 26
Regular (racehorse) 175
Rheims 24, 50, 140
Rhine Valley 136
Ridgeway (Mr) Headmaster,
    St Peter's Court 41

Index

Rifles, 60th 4
Ripley, Surrey 173
Road & Track magazine 90
Rothschild, Guy de 117-8
Rothschild, Philippe de 49-50, 117
Rothschild, Philippine de 50
Rowe & Pitman 186, 189
Rowing 45-6
Royal Ascot (*see* Ascot Racecourse)
Royal Devon and Exeter Hospital 38
Royal Navy Volunteer Reserve 130
Royal St George's Golf Club 4, 43
Royal Tournament 62-3
Royal Wiltshire Yeomanry 27
Ruinart, Nicolas 50
Ruinart, Rheims 50
Russia 4-5
Russian Turkestan 5
Rutland, Duke of 78
Rutland Gate (see Cobbold, Nicholas, homes)

Safe, Mrs (shop owner) 16-17
Salisbury 14, 16, 27, 33, 71
Salisbury Racecourse 176
Salt, Ron 127, 142-3, 149-50
Sana'a, Yemen 112
Sandhurst 24, 26
Sandwich 44
Sarawak 51-2
SAS 99-100
Saudi Arabia 99, 113-6

Scots Guards 7, 147
Scottish Unionist Party 82, 95-6
Seattle 183-4
Sebag 65
Seymour Walk (*see* Cobbold, Nicholas, homes)
Shackleton, Edward 95
Shaw, Liza 131-2
Sheffield, Reggie 87
Sheffield, Robert Charles 40, 87
Shelburne, Lord 171
Shelley, John Frederick 35
Shepherd's Bush 64
Sherman (tank) 26
Shobrooke Park Mansion 35-42, 134, 208
Shorncliffe 73, 75
Shrewsbury School 45
Sibu, Sarawak 51
Silver City Airways 89
Silverstone 129
Sinai Desert 59
Sion Airport 137
Slough 8
Smiley, David 95, 100, 112, 114
Solent, The 76
Solent Road School 17
Somerton-Rayner, Mike 148-50
Somme, Battle of the 6, 52
Sotheby's 8-9
Soudan Road (*see* Cobbold, Nicholas, homes)
South Africa 5, 7-8, 189
South Cerney Airfield 151-3
Southampton 16, 20

Southern Command, Wilton 20, 32
Southover, Tolpuddle 42-3
Southover School, Lewes 42
Soviet Union 99
Spain 109-10, 117, 195
Special Operations Executive 95
Spitfire (aeroplane) 21
St George's Chapel, Windsor 51
St James' Palace 61
St Katherine's Dock 142, 143, 144
St Mary's Calne (school) 166-8
St Mawes 133
St Mawgan RAF Base 133
St Moritz 79
St Moritz Tobogganing Club 79-81
St Peter's Court School 33-42, 44
St Tropez 93
Stalag XI-B (POW camp) 24-5
Stanley (stockbrokers) 92
Stansted Airport 58
Starkey, Greville 175-6
Staverton Airport 126
Stavordale, Lord 10, 33
Stephenson Cobbold (see Cobbold, Nicholas, career)
Stevens, Lord 199-201
Stewart, Jackie 128-9
Stirling, David 99
Stock Exchange 67-8, 183
Stonehall, Great Mongeham 44
Stonehenge 130
Stourhead 130
Sturford Mead, Longleat 27, 28

Sudairi, Zaid 113, 115-6
Sudan 7
Sudeley 130
Suez Canal 57-60, 72, 75
Sunday Express 199-200
Swindon 151
Switzerland 79, 124, 134, 136-7
Sykes, Lavender 10

Talbot Rice, Mr 165-6
Tatler, The 9
Telegraph, The 205
Thames, River 134, 145, 148-50
Thatcher, Margaret 183, 199
The Quiet Don (racehorse) 175-7
Theale, Berkshire 69-70, 121
Thirsk Racecourse 176-7
Throckmorton family 129
Thynne family 27, 31
Thynne, Alexander 27
Thynne, Caroline 27, 28
Thynne, Christopher 27, 28-30, 33, 63, 68-9, 76
Tiger Moth (aeroplane) 69-70
Times, The 88
Tiverton 39
Todhunter family 128
Tolpuddle 42
Topsham 39
Toulouse 186-8
Tours 140
Towcester 129
Tower of London 61, 62
Trawsfynydd, Wales 56
Trimley, Suffolk 111

Index

Tristan and Isolde (opera) 93
Trooping the Colour 61
Tulliemet, Perthshire 106

Uganda 7
United Business Media 201-2
United Nations 73
United News & Media 199-202
United States of America 99, 195
US Air Force 138
US Army 28
Uys (Boer soldier) 8

Vandeleur family 7-8
Vandeleur, Evelyn Norah 8, 10, 11-5, 17-9, 21, 30-1, 32-3, 111
Vandeleur, Seymour 7-8, 53
Venice 186-7
Vicarage Gardens (*see* Cobbold, Nicholas, homes)
Victoria, Queen 9, 33
Vietnam War 124
Vincent, Joseph 46-7
Vivian, Lord 30

Wagner, Richard 93
Walsh, Willie 183
Wandsworth Bridge 149
Warburg 202
Ward, Georgie 9
Warminster 27
Warwick Castle 129-30
Wattisham, RAF 139
Wellington Barracks 61
Wendling, Erhard 198-9

Wentworth Woodhouse 101, 142, 150, 170
Wernher, Julius 5
Westminster, Duke of 55-6
Westminster School 82
Westwood, King's Langley 106
Weymouth, Lady 27
Weymouth, Lord 10, 27
Wheeler, Mavis 30
Wheeler, Mortimer 30
White Waltham (airfield) 69
White's (club) 96, 99-100, 112-3, 173-4, 196
Wiler, Switzerland 134, 136-7
Wilkinson, Elizabeth 3
Williams, Bob 78
Williams de Broë (see Cobbold, Nicholas, career)
Willoughby, Christopher 64
Wilmot-Sitwell, Peter 64-5, 86, 128, 148, 186
Wilton 32, 110, 130
Winchester School 4
Windsor 51, 71
Windsor Hospital 71
World War I 6, 51-2, 112
World War II 1-2, 10-1, 17, 20-8, 42-3, 51-3, 57, 82, 95, 178
Worms (*see* Cobbold, Nicholas, career)
Worms, Nicholas 189-90
Wrightson Wood (*see* Cobbold, Nicholas, career)
Wyecliff, Hay-on-Wye 178
Wyndham, Humphrey 43

Wyndham, Mary 43, 86
Wyndham, Michael 43
Wynyard 102-3, 105
Wyoming 10

Yealm, River 88
Yemen 98-100, 112-5
Yeovil Hospital 47
Yorkshire County Cricket Club 33
Yorkshire Television 200
Yugoslav Lloyd (shipping company) 82

Zippo (whippet) 150